D1565157

# HOW I BECAME A HINDU

By the same author:

*The Myth of the Aryan Invasion of India*
*Hinduism: The Eternal Tradition (Sanatana Dharma)*
*Arise Arjuna: Hinduism and the Modern World*
*Awaken Bharata: A Call for India's Rebirth*

# HOW I BECAME A HINDU

## MY DISCOVERY OF VEDIC DHARMA

DAVID FRAWLEY
(VAMADEVA SHASTRI)

VOICE OF INDIA
New Delhi

© David Frawley
First published, 2000
First reprint, 2000
Second reprint, 2003

ISBN 81-85990-60-3

Published by Voice of India, 2/18, Ansari Road, New Delhi – 110 002.
Printed at Rajkamal Electric Press, Delhi – 110 033.

# Contents

# Foreword

We live in the age of science. The frontiers of our knowledge are receding everyday. The method of science is empirical: it uses experiment to verify or to refute. Science has dispelled miracles from the physical world and it has shown that physical laws are universal. Technology has made astonishing advances and a lot that was the stuff of religious imagination has been brought under the ambit of science. Why should we then be interested in the subject of conversion to Hinduism? Isn't this the age of questioning old-style religion in the manner of *Why I am not a Christian* by the great British philosopher, Bertrand Russell, or the more recent *Why I am not a Muslim* by Ibn Warraq?

David Frawley's remarkable spiritual autobiography answers this question and many more. In a fascinating narrative, he walks us through his own discovery of how the stereotype of Hinduism presented by schoolbooks as a tradition of worship of many gods, social inequity, and meaningless ritual is false. Not that there are not social problems in Hindu society, but these problems are a result of historical processes, India's political and economic vicissitudes of the last few centuries, and not central to the essence of Hinduism. Apart from this and, more significantly, he provides us a portrait of living Hinduism as mirrored by his own life experience.

A unique feature of Hinduism is that it is not obsessed with any specific historical event. Consequently, feality to a 'prophet' is not part of the core belief of the tradition. Rather, the objective is to chart out a path of self-discovery, transformation and knowledge. This path requires constant self-study and validation of experience using common sense and logic.

The traditions of Hinduism may appear as a bewildering complexity to the uninitiated, but the essence of it has great coherence and simplicity. The best way to characterize Hinduism (Sanātana Dharma, the Way of Eternal Truth) is as the science of spirituality. Hindus believe that Brahman (immanent and transcendent God) is the bridge across the ordinary divide of matter and mind. To know oneself one needs to know the expressions of the spirit in all its forms of creative embodiment, which is why devotion to knowledge and truth has diverse forms.

Just as there can be only one outer science, so there can be only one inner science of the spirit. One can only speak of levels of knowledge and understanding. The dichotomy of believers and non-believers, where the believers are rewarded in paradise and the non-believers suffer eternal damnation in hell, is naive. Also, since the physical universe itself is a manifestation of the divine, the notion of guilt related to our bodily existence is meaningless.

Modern science, having mastered the outer reality, has reached the frontier of brain and mind. We comprehend the universe by our minds, but what is the nature of the mind? Are our descriptions of the physical world ultimately no more than a convoluted way of describing aspects of the mind – the instrument with which we see the outer world? Why don't the computing circuits of the computer develop self-awareness as happens in the circuitry of the brain? Why do we have free-will when science assumes that all systems are bound in a chain of cause-effect relationships?

Academic science has no answers to these questions and it appears that it never will. On the other hand, Vedic science focuses on precisely these conundrums. And it does so by gracefully reconciling outer science to inner truth. By seeing the physical universe to be a manifestation of the transcendent spirit, Hindus find meditation on any aspect of this reality to be helpful in the acquisition of knowledge. But Hindus also declare that the notion that the universe consists of just the material reality to be false. Here Hindus are in the company of those scientists who believe that to understand reality one needs recognize consciousness as a principle that complements matter.

We cannot study the outer in one pass; we must look at different portions of it and proceed in stages. Likewise, we cannot know the spirit in one pass; we must look at different manifestations of it and meditate on each to deepen understanding. There can be no regimentation in this practice. Hinduism, by its very nature, is a dharma of many paths. Thomas Jefferson would have approved. He once said, "Compulsion in religion is distinguished peculiarly from compulsion in every other thing. I may grow rich by an art I am compelled to follow; I may recover health by medicines I am compelled to take against my own judgment; but I cannot be saved by a worship I disbelieve and abhor." Not a straitjacket of narrow dogma, Hinduism enjoins us to worship any manifestation of the divine to which one is attuned.

Yoga is the practical vehicle of Hinduism and certain forms of it, such as Haṭha Yoga, have become extremely popular all over the world. This has prepared people to understand the deeper, more spiritual, aspects of Yoga, which lead through Vedanta and the Vedas to the whole Hindu tradition.

Hindu ideas were central to the development of transcendentalism in America in the early decades of the 19th century. That movement played a significant role in the self-definition of America. Hindu ideas have also permeated to the popular consciousness in the West – albeit without an awareness of the source – through the works of leading writers and poets. In many ways Americans and other Westerners are already much more Hindu than they care to acknowledge. Consider the modern fascination with spirituality, self-knowledge, environment, multiculturalism; this ground was prepared over the last two hundred years by Hindu ideas.

David Frawley is one of the most prominent Hindus of our times. He has made fundamental contributions to our understanding of the Vedas; he has also written on Ayurveda and other Vedic sciences. Most importantly, he has urged a return to the Vedas as a means to unlock the secrets of the scriptures that followed. He has shown how this key can reveal the meaning behind the exuberant imagination of the Puranas and the Agamas. It also unlocks the mysteries of Hindu ritual.

Frawley has also been at the forefront of questioning the old colonial paradigm within which Indian history and Hindu religion had been situated by nineteenth century Indologists. He has done this through his writings and lectures all over the world. His work shows the way not only for the Westerner who wishes to understand Hinduism but also for those Hindus who know their religion only through the interpretations of the Indologists.

The Gita says, "Both renunciation of works and also their practice lead to the Supreme. But of these to act rather than to renounce is the better path." Frawley's life story is a testimony to this wisdom of following the path of action. Frawley's work is informed by deep meditation and awareness of larger forces of history. He is a modern rishi in the same spirit as Vivekananda and Aurobindo.

Frawley's work has also shown the relevance of the Vedas for the rediscovery of the forgotten past of the Old Religion, pejoratively called paganism. Ancient Hindus, Greeks, Romans, Celts, and Babylonians knew that their religions were essentially the same. As the sole surviving member of the Old Religion, Hinduism provides us many insights to recognize the universality and perenniality of the spiritual quest. David Frawley's discovery of Hinduism for himself has eased the way for others who want to reach the same goal. His life story provides inspiration to all who wish to be reconnected to the wisdom of our ancestors everywhere.

**Subhash Kak**

Baton Rouge, Louisiana, USA
December 15, 1999

# Preface

The following book unfolds an intellectual and spiritual journey from the West to the East such as a number of people have traveled in recent times. This journey moves from the Western world of materialism to the greater universe of consciousness that permeates India and was the basis of her older civilization. As an inner journey it is more pilgrimage to the spiritual heart of India than an outer visit. Yet it is also a story marked by meetings with important people, friends and teachers who connected me with deeper teachings and guided me along the way.

This journey is not only through space but also through time, into the ancient world and its spiritual culture, such as India has maintained better than any country. It is a reencounter with the spiritual roots of humanity that we have long forgotten or denigrated. The book shows how the ancient Vedic world can come alive and touch us today, not only as a relic of the past but as an inspiration for the future. It is a return to the formative stages of humanity, before we directed our energy to the outer world and were still connected with our cosmic origins. Hopefully, the book can help reawaken this original creative vision of the species that holds the key of transformation for our present darker world.

In my books to date I have written little about myself. This book is a departure and is centered on my own life-experience. The book is autobiographical in tone, but it is not so much an account of my personal life as about how certain changes occurred in my psyche. It focuses on an inner transformation that fundamentally altered who I am and changed my perception of both self and world.

In my case I simply didn't build bridges to the East, I crossed over them and left them far behind. I immersed my being in the soul of the East so completely that I almost ceased to be a Westerner, not only in my thoughts but also in my instincts. I moved from a Western intellectual rationality to a deeper cosmic rationality born of Vedic insight, moving from a humanistic to a cosmic logic and sense of cosmic law.

I trace these changes in order to make them accessible for others, should they wish to follow a similar direction. I have recounted my journey and the bridges over which I once traveled, and how I experienced life while I was still on the other side, so that others can take a similar path.

I moved through Western culture to the Yogic culture of India that seemed ever more expansive, enlightened and happy. I sought the source of that tradition in the ancient Vedas, the oldest wisdom teachings of India, which became my spiritual home and in which I found an untapped treasure house of inexhaustible insight. It was a great adventure with many interesting, if not amazing experiences that transcended my earlier worldview and brought me into a new life and consciousness.

But the journey was arduous and quite challenging. I often thought of turning back and actually did so for certain periods of time. I fell down many times but always eventually got up and kept on going. I had to go beyond not only my own personal and family background but beyond my entire culture and education. This involved breaking with well-entrenched ideas, opinions, habits and feelings. I had to disconnect with the world around me and reconnect with a different world within me. Sometimes I felt like a stranger in a strange land, but if I did try to go back to the old world, I quickly left, finding it to have lost depth and meaning.

The result is that I now look at the Vedic tradition from the inside, as part of my family, as part of my very own blood and breath. I don't view Hinduism with the cold eye of an academician or the starry eyes of a curious and gullible Westerner looking for a new fantasy. I view it as our deepest heritage as human and cosmic beings, as divine souls whose destiny is to bring a higher consciousness in to the world. I have become a worker in this field and hope that my contribution encourages others to join this great cause.

For this book I would like to thank my many teachers and friends and the many Hindu organizations that have helped me in this cause. Most are mentioned in the book, but notably B.L. Vashta, K. Natesan, Avadhuta Shastri, Subhash Kak, N.S. Rajaram, Ashok Chowgule, Swami Satyananda, Ram Swarup, Sita Ram Goel and Arun Shourie.

The Vedic tradition and Hindu Dharma belong to all. Those who reject it are still part of it. Those who try to limit it to a particular sect or point of view don't have the full picture. Until we reconnect with such deeper spiritual impulses we must remain immature as a race and have a culture that, however technically advanced, leaves us unhappy and spiritually destitute. Let us counter this negative trend in civilization by looking once more to the noble spiritual origins from which we came!

The Vedas and the Rishis are true and their influence can overcome any obstacles personally or collectively.

May we honor them once again!

**Dr. David Frawley**

Santa Fe, New Mexico, USA
December 16, 1999

# 1

# Introduction:
# Encountering Hindu Dharma

Most of us are familiar with accounts of how a person has changed from one religion to another, becoming a Christian, Muslim or a Buddhist. In the modern world we are coming to recognize pluralism in religion just as in culture, ethnicity or language. There is no more only one true religion for everyone than there is only one true race, language or way of life.

However, going from Christianity to Hinduism is a rarer story, particularly for a Westerner, because Hinduism does not aim at conversion. Many people think that Hinduism does not take new members at all. It is also a more complex tale because Hinduism is not only a religion, but also a culture and, above all, a spiritual path. To enter into Hindu Dharma involves much more than a shift of belief or accepting a new prophet. To really understand Hindu Dharma requires taking on a new way of life, of which religion is only one aspect.

As a pluralistic system Hinduism does not require that we hold to a single belief or savior or give up an open pursuit of truth. This makes the change into Hinduism less dramatic, overt or disruptive to a person's life and for that reason harder to trace. One does not need to make a statement of faith to become a Hindu but simply recognize the importance of dharma.

In my case it was not a question of a quick conversion like accepting Jesus as one's personal savior or surrendering to Allah. Nor was it the result of a concerted effort to convert me by religious preachers speaking of sin or redemption, or of religious intellectuals trying to convince me of the ultimacy of their particular philosophy or theology. It was a personal decision that occurred as the result of a long quest, a finishing touch of an extensive inner search of many years. The word 'conversion' is a misnomer and a term that I dislike. How can we be converted into anything? We can only be who we are. Understanding who we are is the Hindu and Vedic path. It is not about conversion but about self-knowledge and about cosmic knowledge because who we are is linked to the entire universe. Hinduism is not about joining a church but about developing respect for all beings, not only humans but plants and animals as well. It is not about a particular holy book but about understanding our own minds and hearts. It is not about a savior but about discovering the Divine presence within us.

For most people in the West becoming a Hindu resembles joining a tribal religion, a Native American or Native African belief with many gods and strange rituals, rather than converting to a creed or belief of an organized world religion. Discovering Hinduism is something primeval, a contacting of the deeper roots of nature, in which the spirit lies hidden not as an historical creed but as a mysterious and unnamable power. It is not about taking on another monotheistic belief but an entirely different connection with life and consciousness than our Western religions provide us.

**The Hindu Tradition**

Hinduism is the oldest religion in the world with a tradition going back to the very beginning of what we know of as history over five thousand years ago. It is the third largest of the world's religions, with nearly a billion members or one-sixth of humanity. It is the largest non-Biblical or, to use a pejorative term, Pagan tradition remaining today. As such it holds the keys to the pre-Christian beliefs that all cultures once had and many people still retain.

Hinduism is the world's largest pluralistic tradition. It believes in many paths and recognizes many names and forms for God, both masculine and feminine. It contains many sages, many scriptures and many ways to know God. Its emphasis is not on mere belief as constituting salvation but on union with the Divine as the true goal of life.

Hinduism is a culture containing its own detailed traditions of philosophy, medicine, science, art, music and literature that are quite old, venerable and intricate. It is the foundation of Indian culture that is rooted in the Sanskrit language which first arose as Hinduism's sacred language. Most importantly, Hinduism is a great spiritual path with Yogic traditions of meditation, devotion and insight, in which religion in the outer sense of ritual and prayer is only secondary. Its wealth of teachings on mantra, meditation, *prāṇa*, *kuṇḍalini*, *chakras* and Self-realization is perhaps unparalleled in the world.

Because of its cultural and spiritual sides some people say that Hinduism is not a religion but a way of life. Yet though it is a way of life Hinduism is also a religion in the sense that it teaches about God and the soul, karma and liberation, death and immortality. It has its holy books, temples, pilgrimage sites, and monastic orders like other major world religions.

Hindus have a deep faith in their religion and its traditions. Thousands if not millions of Hindus have died for their religion in the many holy wars that have targeted them over the last more than a thousand years. They refused to convert even when faced with threats of death and torture. Both Islam and Christianity found converting Hindus to be particularly difficult, not because Hindus responded to assaults on their religion with force, but because their faith in their own religion and its great yogis was unshakeable.

The Western mind characteristically downplays Hinduism's importance as a religion. In many contemporary studies of world religions Hinduism is left out altogether. Because it has no overriding one God, single historical founder, or set creed,

Hinduism is looked upon as a disorganized collection of cults. Few Westerners know what Hinduism is, or what Hindus believe and practice. Most are content with negative stereotypes that make them feel comfortable about their own religions. If Hinduism is mentioned in the Western media it is relative to disasters, conflicts or backward social customs. It is the one religion that is still politically correct to denigrate, if not belittle.

There is also a general impression that Hinduism is closed, ethnic or castist creed and therefore not a true world religion. This is strange because historically Hinduism spread throughout South Asia and specific ways of becoming a Hindu are described in many Hindu teachings. Hinduism could not have spread so far if it was not expansive in bringing in new members.

Many Hindus seem to confirm these ideas. A number of Hindu teachers say that they will make a Christian a better Christian or a Muslim a better Muslim, as if Hinduism had nothing better or unique to offer. They often apologize about being Hindus when asked about their religion. They say, "Yes I am a Hindu, but I accept all other religions as well," which includes religions that do not accept Hinduism!

Some Hindu temples, particularly in South India, will not allow Westerners, that is people of lighter skin color, to enter even if they have already formally become Hindus. Other Hindus simply don't know how to communicate their tradition. The result is that the more universal or liberal aspects of Hinduism are forgotten. Or they go by another name in the West as Yoga, Vedanta or the teachings of a particular guru, in which case they can become popular all over the world as many modern spiritual movements have demonstrated.

### Discovering Hinduism through the Vedas

In my case I came to Hindu Dharma through the Vedas, the oldest tradition of Hinduism. This was an unusual way because the Vedas are so old that most Hindus know little about them, following instead more recent teachings. People in the West have no real idea what the Vedas are either. They see Hinduism through a few prominent images like Shiva, Krishna and the Goddess or a few famous modern gurus and are not aware of the older foundation of this multifarious tradition. Most Hindus know their particular sect or guru but have little recognition of their tradition and its long history.

Even Hindus who speak of the glory of the Vedas generally can't explain Vedic teachings in detail. By the Vedas they usually mean the Upanishads or the *Bhagavad-gītā*, not the older Vedic texts. Western academia believes that the Vedas are only primitive poetry, tribal rites, or some strange babbling that arose from shamanic intoxications. At best, for the more spiritually enlightened, the Vedas are regarded as the lesser growths from which the greater unfoldments of Yoga and Vedanta arose or diverged.

For me, however, the Vedas became revealed not only as the source of the Hindu tradition but as the core spiritual wisdom of humanity. I could say that I am more a Vedic person, a Vedicist if your will, than simply a Hindu in the ordinary sense. This might better describe what I think to the modern world. But I can't draw a line between Hinduism and Vedic Dharma, though some people might try to.

## Overcoming Anti-Hindu Stereotypes

Hinduism is a religion with many Gods and Goddesses, with strange images of many heads, many arms or animal features. It teems with magic and mysticism, with gurus and godmen and their miraculous powers and enlightened insight. Much of this appears erotic or even violent to us, accustomed as we are to no images in religious worship or to only a few holy images like Christ on the cross or the Madonna with her child. Hinduism appears like a form of brainwashing or mind control, a cultish religion with little to offer a rational and humane Western mind.

This negative idea of Hinduism is shaped by missionary and colonial propaganda that we have been bombarding India with for centuries. Hindus continue to be among the main targets of world missionary efforts. The missionaries highlight the poor, sick and outcasts of India as needing salvation – the victims of a backward religion that we must help them escape from. We focus on the poverty of India today as the measure of the Hindu culture and religion, emphasizing, if not promoting social problems in India as a means of encouraging conversion. Were we to be conquered by a foreign power in the future and become a poor country, I wonder how many of our poor people would convert to the conqueror's religion for material benefit just as we have long encouraged others to do?

It is amazing how little credit we in the West give to other cultures and religions such as the Hindu. Is our denigration of such different and ancient practices a reflection of a real perception or the shadow of our own arrogance? Why do we see our religions as necessarily better, though religion is hardly a real concern for most of us, or if it is a concern, is little more than a missionary cult, not any profound mysticism or philosophy?

We haven't looked at Hinduism directly but have blindly followed a jaded vision of it. Hinduism is a free and open culture encouraging self-realization. Its diversity is born of this creativity, not of mere superstition. It is much more like the global culture we aspire to in our spiritual moments, rather than what we would look back upon as the mud from which we came.

Encountering Hinduism, therefore, means questioning our very idea of what religion should be. Hinduism is overflowing with variety and even contradiction. One could say that there are more religions inside of Hinduism than outside of it. Everything that we find in human religious activity from aboriginal rites to insights of pure consciousness is already there in the great plethora of Hindu teachings and practices.

Hinduism is not only connected with many Gods but with the formless absolute – the mysterious immutable Brahman beyond not only the Gods and Goddesses, but even beyond the Creator. It has a place for monotheism but regards monotheism as only one aspect of human religious experience, not the measure of it all.

Hinduism accepts all human approaches to religion, including its rejection, being willing to accept atheists into its fold. It does not try to circumscribe the abundance of life in any formula. It can even accept Christianity as another line of religious experience but not as the only one or necessarily the best.

Hinduism is not passed on by memorizing a creed, though it does have clearly defined and highly articulate teachings and philosophies. It is intimately connected with the Earth, nature, society and our daily activities from eating and breathing to sleeping and dying. Hindu Dharma sees itself not as manmade but as part of cosmic creation, an emanation of the cosmic mind. It aligns us with the cosmic religion that exists in all worlds and at all times. It is a way to link with the cosmic life, not a belief that we can retreat into like a shell or like a fortress.

## The Question of Becoming a Hindu

Why would anyone, particularly a modern and educated person born in the West, want to become a Hindu, much less feel proud in calling himself one? How could a person find value in the primitive Vedic roots of this ambiguous religion? After all, the term Hindu connotes an ethnic religion mired in caste, idolatry, and the oppression of women. It appears anti-modern, inhumane, if not embarrassing for those who would follow it.

A forward thinking person could not take on such an identity, or could he? Is it a mere seeking of emotional security? Indeed, many intellectuals out of their own doubts, perhaps an inherent emotional weakness of the intellectual mind, have embraced regressive creeds. Intellectual apologists can be found for every strange ideology. Even Hitler and Stalin had them. So praise for an ideology or religion even by an intelligent person cannot be taken without skepticism.

At the same time we cannot ignore the fact that there is much in the world that goes beyond our current cultural preconceptions. We are beginning to appreciate the deeper meaning of myths and symbols, which Hinduism abounds in. We are gaining a new respect for meditation and Yoga to reach a higher awareness beyond the pale of religious dogma. We are recognizing the distortions born of Eurocentrism and Western materialism and revising our estimate of native cultures. That we might have to revise our ideas of Hinduism from colonial, missionary or Marxist perceptions is without doubt.

Yet even those who have embraced Indic spiritual traditions like Yoga generally find the appellation of being a Hindu to be unappealing. Being a Buddhist, a Christian or a Muslim seems more universal, even recognizing that these traditions may lack the diversity and richness of Hinduism. The term Hinduism has become quite tainted and seldom connotes anything high or noble to the mass mind.

In addition many enlightened thinkers, particularly from India, believe that we should go beyond all outer identities whether cultural, national or religious. After all, our true nature is not Hindu, Christian, American, Russian, or anything else. We are all human beings with the same basic urges and inclinations. So why have any religious identity at all? The age of religions is over and we should be entering an age of spiritual search without boundaries.

Such thinking misses the point that Hinduism is not a credal religion based upon a person, institution or dogma. Hindu Dharma welcomes the spiritual search without boundaries. In fact, its great variety of teachings and methods provides a good foundation for a free individual search, which otherwise as an isolated effort may not go far, just as free inquiry in science benefits from a broad and open tradition of science to draw from. Most people in the world are not at the level of high spiritual practices or ready to renounce the world. They need religious teachings, including prayers and rituals to shape their work, social and family lives on an ethical and devotional level. But such religious teachings should be broad based, containing something for all aspects of society and connected to the highest truth as well. Hindu Dharma provides all this in a powerful way.

We should not forget the facts of our individual existence and the organic connections of our lives. Each one of us has a certain life span. We live in a certain place and partake of a certain culture. We have our particular temperament and individual inclinations. All this shapes who we are and how we approach the higher Self. Only a rare soul can transcend the influence of time and even he or she must consider the forces of time, just as one cannot avoid being affected by the food that one eats.

The Yoga tradition considers that unless a person has purity in body and mind he cannot transcend them. Similarly, unless we have harmony in our culture and life-style it is very difficult to go beyond them. Unless we have a culture that supports the spiritual life, few will be able to pursue it. Culture is the soil on which we grow like a plant to open out into the boundless sky. We cannot ignore nurturing the soil of culture in our seeking of the unlimited beyond. Hinduism with its broad spiritual culture offers this ground on which to grow. It contains the abundant creative forces and variety of nature itself.

Unfortunately, certain religions hold that they alone are true and that other religions are unholy or dangerous. This divisive and exclusive idea of religion is the real problem, not religion per se, which is a necessary part of human culture. Yet this narrow idea of religion has so dominated the

Western world that most people take it for granted as representing what religion really is, which makes Hinduism with all of its diversity seem almost incomprehensible. Religion, in the original meaning of the word, means to link together. It should provide us tools for self-realization, enabling us to unfold our full divine potential. In this process we will probably need to follow a certain teaching, with specific disciplines and practices. We cannot follow all religions any more than we can eat all food or perform all jobs. We will probably also become part of a spiritual group or family. We cannot have everyone as a mother or father. We usually have our lineage and our transmission in the spiritual life, just as in other aspects of life. Indeed such connections are more important in the spiritual life because spirituality is more intimate, more interior and less capable of being transmitted in an outer, mechanical or mass-produced way than other aspects of culture.

Some people argue that the name Hindu is inappropriate because it is not traditional. After all the great Rishis and Yogis didn't call themselves Hindus but simply spoke of truth and dharma. The reason for this lack of definition is that Hinduism is an open tradition. It is not defined versus an Other as are Biblical traditions that reflect a dichotomy of Christian-pagan or Muslim-*kāfir*. Many Hindus have only become conscious of being Hindu because of the negativity they have encountered from Christians and Muslims trying to convert them.

Sanātana Dharma or the universal dharma is a more correct term and reflects the broader basis of the Hindu tradition. Unfortunately, it is cumbersome and unfamiliar. The terms "dharmic" and "native" traditions are also helpful because Hinduism grows out of the land and is connected with life itself. But Hinduism is the convenient term, whatever limitations may be associated with it. So we must define it in an appropriate manner. This is to face our own prejudices about Hinduism, which are probably more deep-seated than we would think. Why should we object to the term Hindu for such a broad tradition, while accepting the names for much narrower religions?

This prejudice against the Hindu religion reflects a built-in prejudice against non-Biblical beliefs. The Western pattern of religion as one true faith, along with a missionary effort, is used as the standard for all proper religion. Missionary aggression is associated with universality in belief, while tolerant religions that see no need to convert the world are condemned as merely ethnic or tribal beliefs.

Buddhism is more respected than Hinduism in the West because it at least has the one historical Buddha to relate to and a more homogenous and missionary type tradition. Buddhism can be placed in the Western model of religion, but without a Creator. Hinduism, on the other hand, calls up all our misconceptions about religion. For that reason it is a good place to enlarge our views and gain a greater understanding of our global religious heritage, most of which does not lie in Western monotheism.

In my case I came to Hindu Dharma after an earlier exploration of Western intellectual thought and world mystical traditions, a long practice of Yoga and Vedanta and a deep examination of the Vedas. In the process I came into contact with diverse aspects of Hindu society and with Hindu teachers that few Westerners have access to, taking me far beyond the range of the usual perceptions and mis-conceptions about the subject. Such direct experience, which was often quite different than what I had expected or was told would be the case, changed my views and brought me to my current position. Hopefully my story can help others change from taking Hinduism as something primitive to understanding the beauty of this great spiritual tradition that may best represent our spiritual heritage as a species.

# 2

# Early Years: Growing Up
# Out of Catholicism

I always had a certain mystical sense, going back to early childhood. Whether it was looking at the sky and gazing at the clouds or seeing distant snow covered mountains, I knew in my heart that there was a higher consciousness behind the world. I felt a sacred and wonderful mystery from which we had come and to which we would return after our short sojourn on this strange planet.

The human world seemed like a confined sphere, a prison filled with conflict and suffering, marked by the clash of human emotions, shifting desires and instinctual needs. But beyond was a wide and beneficent universe with open arms ready to embrace us if we would but set aside our human compulsions. The question was how to reach that other realm or if it were even possible while we are alive and active in this vale of sorrow. Though one could glimpse that higher realm in quiet moments there was always the travail of the human world in which one had to live, which seemed inescapable.

I had trouble reconciling this mystical sense with the idea of religion that I contacted through my Catholic background. Both my parents grew up on dairy farms in the Midwest of the United States (Wisconsin) and came from strong Catholic backgrounds. My mother's family in particular was quite pious and a pillar of the Church where they lived, following all the Church observances and donating liberally to its causes. One of her brothers was a priest, a missionary in

South America, and he was regarded very highly, pursuing a very noble and holy occupation.

Generally one son in the family would become a priest. My mother thought that I would become the priest in our family. I did have a religious disposition and for most of my childhood tried to be pious, but somehow I couldn't really connect with the Church or its beliefs, which were as frightening as they were appealing. With their trappings of suffering, sin and guilt Catholic beliefs seemed more part of the human world rather than that other magical realm where human turbulence couldn't enter.

My parents were the first generation off the farm in the post-war era and came to live in the city. Because of their Catholic background, which at that time was against any form of contraception, they were compelled to have many children like their parents. Many children in the city didn't mean more helpers as on the farm but only more mouths to feed and more expenses for education. My mother had ten children by the time she was thirty-five, with a new baby every two years. I was the second child, born when she was twenty-one. I had one elder brother, seven younger sisters and one younger brother. The family size inevitably led us into financial difficulty. My parents were the first casualties of the Church mind that I would soon come to oppose.

The most memorable events as a child were our weekend visits to my grandparent's farm (on my mother's side), which was still in the old world and almost European. They had a huge house, as well as a big farm with barns, cows and a wide pasture. They had large dinners, holiday gatherings and a sense of family togetherness extending through several generations. Though our lives gradually moved away from this traditional Catholic religious background, it was there at the beginning and foundation of my life. It lingers here and there in my dreams, like a shadow out of which I gradually emerged.

## Younger Years as a Catholic

I attended Catholic school until the fifth grade or about the age of ten years old (I was born in 1950). I tried to be devout, attending mass, doing prayers and following the commandments. I shied away from being an altar boy, however, feeling nervous about appearing in public. The sense of Catholic guilt, however, was enormous and came to block my piety.

We were taught of venal and mortal sins. Venal sins would land us in purgatory where we would be summarily tortured, but the suffering, however bad, would eventually come to an end. Mortal sins would take us to an eternal hell from which there was no possible redemption. Venal sins were generally simple things like disobeying one's parents or teachers. Mortal sins were another matter. Some mortal sins were obvious criminal acts, like robbery or killing a person, which violate all sense of ethics and fellow feeling. Other mortal sins, however, consisted of a merely ignoring of Church injunctions like missing church on Sunday, missing confession or the other sacraments. By the first standard I shouldn't go to hell. By the second I had missed some Church obligations so I was definitely a candidate for the eternal fires.

Children take such punishment threats quite seriously, particularly those who are more sensitive. In retrospect we can perhaps laugh at them as strict ways of training children, like a strong stake for a young tree, but their effect on a child's psyche should not be underestimated. Perhaps being sensitive I was more inclined to believe such injunctions, but after all, didn't they come from God and his holy Church?

Going to confession was another great fear of mine. The problem was that I was afraid to tell the priest my sins, thinking that they were much worse than they actually were. I felt that I was probably the only or the worst offender of religious rules. I didn't seem to notice that I was more pious than the other children were, including my brothers and sisters. I also did the usual childhood pranks, like irritating the nuns who taught us, which I felt were probably mortal sins as well. The result was that I didn't confess all my sins and my guilt got worse. I also felt that the sins got worse, though in retrospect my real failing was taking such religious rules seriously at all.

I remember doing prayers to atone for my little sins, which seemed like major soul failings at the time. These prayers were called "indulgences" and allowed us to get rid of our potential punishment after death. Each prayer would say something like "good for two hundred days in purgatory," meaning that its recitation would save a person from that amount of suffering after death. My problem was that I couldn't figure out exactly how much time in purgatory my sins merited. But at least it promised a way to eradicate my sins without having to announce all my dastardly deeds to the priest. Yet it didn't deal with the greater problem of my few mortal sins which weighed on me and caused much worry and anxiety. Later the Church ended this business of indulgences and no longer prescribed time off of purgatory for its prayers. I doubt that God was informed that the Church changed his laws. But that came long after I left the Church.

Of course there were the usual childhood activities, with sports in school and the general issues of growing up that brought about their own joys and stresses, but the Catholic religion loomed behind with its strange doctrines, threats and demands, spoiling the innocence and happiness of childhood. No doubt it has done this for many children throughout the world, who then as adults feel compelled to perpetuate the same abuse on their own children in the name of becoming good Christians.

Another question I had was, if belief in Jesus and following the ways of the Church guaranteed that one would go to heaven, why should one make any effort beyond it? What was the need for any extreme piety or saintliness? The nuns told me two things. First the usual purgatory idea, that even minor sins had great punishments, though not in hell. Second, if one was particularly good one got a bigger house in heaven, with saints having great mansions. I wasn't quite certain what a house in heaven might be, and the whole thing seemed suspicious. And what would one do for eternity in heaven, which sounded like a glorification of life on earth?

I always pondered about things and never merely accepted them at face value. I tried to figure out why something is so and what it really means. As a child I began to think about religion as well. I soon realized that we are supposed to take religious matters as articles of faith, which means to be quiet and accept them, however odd they may appear. Such faith is usually a veil for our human needs or for superstitions that cannot stand scrutiny. I couldn't suppress myself from thinking in the name of faith in something, like the miracles of Jesus, which had little to do with me and seemed impossible.

The figure of Jesus on the cross that we saw during mass was rather gruesome and unpleasant. One didn't want to look at it. We were told that we had all killed Jesus. We were responsible for his death by our sins, which were terrible in the eyes of God. But then I never knew Jesus and since he lived two thousand years ago, how could my actions have affected him? I could never really relate to the image of the sacrificed savior who saves us, we who cannot save ourselves. I also began to notice that we all have our personal failings, including the nuns that taught us who had evident tempers and not much patience. The whole thing didn't seem to be as God given as we were told it was.

The Christian God who had to sacrifice his own son to save humanity was a figure of both fear and enigma. This strange God created the Devil as well. And of course we were all afraid of the Devil and his retinue, particularly at night or on Halloween. This strange God was distant and unapproachable and yet demanded so much of his creatures.

He had to allow his only begotten son to be killed. With all his omniscience one would think that he could have done better with his own creation or better helped his Church. The idea of a personal God who dispensed rewards and punishments seemed more like some irrational despot than any sense of the transcendent.

Yet religion offered some means of access to that other mystical world, or at least I thought that it did. Christmas with its dark snowy nights and the birth of the Divine child had something fascinating that kept my mind and heart attracted. So though my faith was disturbed I still held on to it, hoping that something better would come from it.

I remember first encountering Protestants, or rather realizing that the people nearby followed a dangerous religious heresy. The Church taught us that Protestants were deluded Christians who were all going to hell. Protestants denied the authority of the Church and the infallibility of the pope, which were not to be questioned by a good Christian. At first I was hesitant to associate with them, feeling bad for their plight, wondering how much they would suffer in hell. I was suspicious about them as if they had some sort of plague.

But boys will be boys and play games together, regardless of their family faiths. Later I learned that Protestants were human beings like we Catholics and, as boys to boys were just other friends. These great religious divides, like strict religious rules, appeared manmade or part of a special world outside of life that people found it convenient to ignore. I began to realize that for all the talk of heaven and hell that most people, including my parents, really didn't take religion very seriously.

I was a bit intellectually precocious as a child. At the age of nine I began avidly reading biographies of great men. I don't remember who they all were today but I recall noting that they came from various ethnic, racial and religious backgrounds. My training that only Catholics had a monopoly on goodness was already getting a severe drubbing. Clearly greatness depended more upon conduct than upon creed, more upon character than on belief.

I remember one experience in particular when I was about ten. We lived in La Crosse, Wisconsin, a small city on the Mississippi River. One day my brother and I were walking on the ice of the river, which froze over in the winter. He dared me to walk near a hole in the ice. Being not only daring but also foolish I took a few steps towards the hole and suddenly fell through the ice. Fortunately, I was able to pull myself back up onto the ice or I would have surely drowned. This shocked me and produced a moment of introspection in which my entire life flashed before me.

After walking home I happened to see a television program on the Maya Indians of Central America and their strange rituals. I felt that this was a world that would be important to me for the future. I had undergone some sort of initiation and was ready for a new life. We moved to Denver, Colorado, shortly thereafter and never again returned to the Midwest. While we had already lived in Colorado for brief periods before this time we had always returned to Wisconsin and I had previously not escaped the influence of my Catholic world there. Now that world would pass away.

In the American West I came into contact with the beauty of the Rocky Mountains and felt their mystical power. I transferred my devotion to these snowy peaks. Catholicism for me was mainly of the Midwest, the farmhouse and my grandparents. In Colorado the beauty of nature and the mountains dominated over the Church, which seemed out of place in the greater universe where there are no manmade boundaries.

## Science and History/Leaving the Church

We moved at first to the suburbs in Denver, which was a big city. Unlike the small towns in which we had mainly lived, it opened me up to broader cultural influences. This was particularly so since, owing to financial constraints, we had to enter public school for the first time. The public schools removed me from religious indoctrination. My mind grew under new stimulation.

At first we were wary of public school, because in parochial (Catholic) school we were taught that public school was dangerous. It was irreligious, didn't teach about God, and allowed people to mix regardless of their faiths. I had to learn to compartmentalize religion, forget its rigidities, and just be in school with other children. As school children it seemed to matter little what our religious background was and it was seldom a topic of discussion or consideration.

In my first year of public school I became deeply interested in science, particularly astronomy in which we had a special class that entranced me. The Catholic schools of the time had little by way of science classes. Soon I was reading books on physics, cosmology and relativity. I may not have understood the details but my view of the universe made a radical shift. I began to connect my innate mystical sense with the scientific vastness of a cosmos unbounded by time and space. Compared to these great vistas of science the Catholic Church appeared narrow and backward.

In a couple of years I bought a telescope from the money gained by summer jobs that I had done. Later I got larger telescopes. I spent many hours as a young teenager looking up at the stars at night. It was not just a hobby or an interest in science but part of a mystical quest. It once more gave me a sense of that greater universe of consciousness and the cosmic lights that shimmered behind our semi-darkened world.

I also read many books on science fiction that helped spread my mental horizons and widen my imagination. There were other planets and different types of intelligent life far more advanced than we are and no doubt having higher religions and philosophies as well. Life contained many other possibilities that I was beginning to discover, moving beyond the boundaries of my rigid religious beliefs.

I was always fascinated with history, which public school also had more to offer. At first it was American history that intrigued me, including the settling of the West, about which I sympathized with the Native Americans who seemed more the victims than the aggressors in this continental saga. The history of World War II was a big topic of the then post-war era. This led me to a special study of European history from about the age of fourteen.

Europe had a much broader and more diverse culture and a longer history that drew my curiosity. European history brought me in contact with the history of the Church with its political and military popes and anti-popes. I learned of the many religious wars in Europe like the bloody Thirty Years War in the seventeenth century that resulted in over one third of the population of Germany getting decimated. I learned about the European extermination of the Native Americans under Cortez and Pizarro. I began to see the dark side of my Catholic religion. My lingering religious sentimentality and childhood nostalgia for the Church gradually faded.

Another subject of fascination was geography. From a young age I played with the globe and loved to look over maps of the world, memorizing the countries, their terrain and their cities. I realized that we lived on a large planet composed of many lands with diverse religions and cultures, most of which I was taught little about in school. I was particularly interested in distant and exotic places, as if they contained some key to humanity that I was searching for. I didn't see any need to get the entire world to follow the same religion.

For such reasons at the young age of fourteen I suddenly decided of my own accord to stop going to church on Sundays. At first I just pretended to go and then went somewhere else, like taking a walk in the park. Soon my parent knew that I was no longer interested in the church and gradually accepted it. In fact I led what became a family movement away from the Catholic Church. But at the time I still felt some guilt about the matter. I was not attending church but I had not left its influence entirely behind me either.

At the age of fifteen I had a remarkable schoolteacher who taught a class on ancient history that opened my eyes about the ancient world. The class focused on ancient Egypt, which I found to be utterly fascinating. Out of the enthusiasm so generated I memorized the entire list of the Pharaohs of Egypt and would recite them with pride. I could sense in ancient Egypt a monumental spiritual culture with great inner power and magic. I imagined living at that time, which seemed much more interesting than the modern world in which I was trapped.

This began my fascination with ancient cultures that eventually led me to the Vedas. I sensed that the ancients had a better connection to the universe than we moderns and that their lives had a higher meaning. I gradually studied the ancient history of other lands, particularly ancient Persia, which also had a special pull for me. Clearly the American focus of our education left out most of humanity both in time and space.

## Intellectual Awakening and the Counterculture

About the age of sixteen I underwent a major intellectual awakening. It came as a powerful experience that radically changed my thoughts and perception. Initially it was quite disturbing and disorienting. While some sort of intellectual ferment had been developing in me for several years, this one resulted in a profound break from the authorities and ideas of my childhood and the vestiges of my American education. It initiated a series of studies that encompassed Western intellectual thought and first brought me in contact with Eastern spirituality. It marked an important transition in my life.

At this time I began to write a philosophical type of poetry, which I kept secretly to myself. I lost interest in science and mathematics that had been my main mental pursuits. My interest in Europe became stronger but moved from its history to its thought and culture. America began to seem a rather provincial country, devoid of sophistication or culture. I began to study the writers and intellectuals of modern Europe. This started with Nietzsche and Camus and extended to Sartre, Heidegger and other existentialists. Nietzsche was initially my favorite. His atheism appealed to my anti-Church sentiments. His staunch individualism gave me confidence in my independent views. Plus he had an almost mystic or intoxicated bent that I could relate to.

I looked briefly into rationalist philosophers like Kant, Hegel or Bertrand Russell but was not drawn to them. I found them too dominated by a dry reason that seemed devoid of life and creativity. My mind had a certain emotional or artistic urge and was not content with mere logic or science.

The Existentialists at first stimulated me with their deep questions about consciousness and perception. I began to think about consciousness and how it works. They were rather depressing as well. Emptiness, despair and suicide were ideas I could relate to as part of growing up in a world without meaning, but I was not so morbid in temperament as to be swallowed up by them. Existentialism eventually seemed to me to be a rather dry and hopeless affair. The Existentialists had no solution to the dilemma of existence that they so eloquently pointed out. The atheist Existentialists generally took refuge in Communism. The theistic ones returned to the Church with an irrational leap of faith. But the problem of our inherent nothingness was not something that they had any real method to solve.

The example of the Existentialists showed me that the intellect by itself, however rational or cunning, could not arrive at any ultimate truth. A higher consciousness was required for that. The intellect gets caught in endless doubts and ends in nihilism or agnosticism. Excessive thinking weakens the emotions and saps the will. It didn't take me long to realize that the Existentialists were not going anywhere.

The German existential philosopher Heidegger, however, connected me with the concept of Being, which seemed to be the greatest insight in Existentialism, though generally I found his philosophy to be too complex and verbose. With the idea of Pure Being I felt on a firm ground and knew that a greater truth and peace enveloped the universe, but that the intellect was probably not the right vehicle to understand it.

Once in high school I openly challenged a priest who was giving a talk at the school auditorium criticizing the Existentialists. He used the ignorance of his audience to plant negative ideas about these thinkers so that the students would not fall under their influence. I realized that we should speak out on these issues and not simply be silent or such distortions would go unchallenged. My remarks created a lot of commotion and the priest was shaken. I learned that speaking out can have a strong impact on people.

I became involved in the American counterculture about the same time, hanging out with the local hippies and intellectuals in downtown Denver cafes, spending evenings and weekends there. While I read a lot on my own, getting books from our large public library, I also dialogued extensively with various local intellectuals, striking up new friendships. Several college teachers and area poets helped direct me to new thinkers and writers, including those from Asia. We had various intellectual groups and contacts, generally of an informal nature, that met and freely discussed various artistic and philosophical topics.

I became a counterculture figure in my local high school, which was quite large as it was centered in the downtown region. I lost interest in my school studies that seemed very narrow in their ideas. While I came to school with many books to study, most had little to do with the actual classes that I was taking. Yet because of my intellectual habits the teachers tolerated my eccentricity. My revolt was not simply youthful emotion but had an intellectual thrust, which they found hard to refute. They created a special class for me and for another such intellectual student to address our deeper interests. But we also found this class to be boring. Like the Marxists, whom I would later sympathize with during the anti-war movement, I felt a revolt against the bourgeoisie, specifically the American middle class. I would walk through the array of tract homes in the city and feel what a meaningless life it was, so standardized and mechanical, without any real thinking or creativity. It seemed that everyone was involved in a pursuit of material gain that went nowhere, except to mediocrity. This was not so much a political as an intellectual revolt, though it eventually developed political ramifications.

I revolted against American culture or rather against the lack of it. What had my country really added to civilization apart from mass production and technological inventions? What had it produced in terms of poetry, art, philosophy or literature? I became a kind of expatriate. I wouldn't read or study American authors except for Thoreau. I sympathized with writers like Henry Miller who abandoned the United States for Europe. I felt that American culture was a diminution of a greater European culture for which I had a greater affinity.

## Mystical Poetry and Discovery of Eastern Spirituality

Throughout this intellectual revolt I never lost sight of a higher reality. I fancied myself to be a "mystical atheist" because though I rejected the Biblical idea of a personal God I did recognize an impersonal consciousness or pure being behind the universe. I also remember reading Herman Hesse's *Journey to the East*. I learned that there were great spiritual and mystical traditions in the East that perhaps still existed. I began my own journey to the East.

Meanwhile I also studied European poetry and art. I particularly enjoyed the French symbolist poets like Rimbaud and Mallarme who had a mystic vision. The German mystic poet Rilke, however, was my favorite and best epitomized what I thought real poetry should be. Poetry had a depth and ambiguity that philosophy could not reach. I realized that it was a better vehicle to reflect this mysterious universe in which we live.

I examined twentieth century European artistic movements like the Surrealists and Dadaists as well. While I enjoyed their images and ideas I felt that their style of expression had become crude. I preferred something more classical in art. The modern art of the machine, the newspaper or the mass media seemed vulgar. I could not relate to the degradation found in modern art, particularly what transpired after World War II. I also found that rather than breaking through into a higher perception such artists generally remained trapped in hedonism or got caught in drugs, neurosis, or suicide. They hadn't found a way out either, though perhaps they could look over the walls that confine us.

My own poetry became more imagistic, reflecting a symbolist base like that of Rilke or Rimbaud. Images of the dawn and the night, the sun, wind and fire arose in mind like primordial forces, with vague images of ancient Gods. These poems also had Eastern affinities that I was gradually discovering. They were images of an internal landscape that itself was a doorway into the universe of consciousness and the cosmic powers. Many of these images I would later find in the poetry of Sri Aurobindo and in the *Rigveda*.

In my poetic writings I could sense a feminine archetype or muse guiding and inspiring me. An inherent sense of the Goddess existed inside of me, which took shape in my poems. She was the Divine power hidden in the beauty of nature, which reflected a secret power of consciousness and life. This would later connect me with the Goddess traditions of India.

About the same time I began to study Eastern texts from

Lao Tzu to the Upanishads, which were readily available at the time. I discovered the Hare Krishna, TM and other Eastern groups that were visible in this large western city where I lived. While a more European ethos dominated my mind the Eastern view was not far behind and getting closer. I began to see in these Eastern teachings the answers to the questions that Western intellectuals had failed to achieve. More importantly, they had methods to reach higher states of consciousness, while the intellectual tradition of the West could only conceptualize about it.

I remember once walking down the street and realizing that the sky was Krishna. I intuitively felt that such deities reflected cosmic realities, windows on the universe. I found the idea of Brahma, Vishnu and Shiva as the three great forces of creation, preservation and destruction in the universe to make sense.

Psychology was another interesting topic that I discovered, including Freud's ideas on sex, which helped liberate me from my Catholic background, but I felt that he had not understood the deeper levels of the mind and its creative process. Then I encountered the works of Carl Jung on Psychology and Alchemy, which brought on another revelation. I spent my summer after high school in 1968 not preparing for college but going through Jung's esoteric works on Psychology and Alchemy.

The images that he pointed out – the sun and the lion, the phoenix and the cauldron – were much like the poetic images that I was working with. They brought me in contact with older European mystical traditions. I realized that there was a spiritual current in Europe in spite of the Church, and that it not only used Christian symbols in a spiritual context but retained older Pagan symbols and contacts with the Eastern world. The alchemical tradition was universal and extended even to China. I discovered that symbols were not only poetic images but had a psychological power, an appeal to the collective unconscious, and that they took us in the direction of the ancient Gods and Goddesses.

This led me to a discovery of the Renaissance and its art and philosophy, which I examined in some depth. But it seemed that the Renaissance went the wrong way. It started off as a mystical awakening with Marsilio Ficino and a translation of hermetic works, but soon got caught in realism and materialism. The West had moved away from the rigidity of the Church but only to the other extreme of materialism, not to a real discovery of the Spirit that could reconcile both true religion and true science.

Out of curiosity from my Catholic background, I looked into Thomas Aquinas and Catholic philosophy as well. It seemed rather dry and dogmatic and had little mysticism in it. The teachings of mystical Christianity through the teachings of Meister Eckhart made more sense and I moved on to these. For a while I tried to get back into Christianity outside of the pale of the Church, perhaps out of some personal nostalgia. But it quickly became clear to me that the mystical Christian tradition consisted of incomplete teachings or isolated individuals, a tradition that had been crushed before it could flower.

The law of karma and the process of rebirth that I had learned about through Eastern philosophy made more sense to me than such Christian teachings. After reading a number of different scriptures and spiritual texts from all over the world, the Christian fixation on Jesus seemed almost neurotic. It was clear to me that there have been many great sages throughout history and Jesus, however great, was only one of many and that his teachings were not the best preserved either. I failed to see what was so unique about him or what his teachings had that could not be found with more clarity elsewhere. The mystic feeling I once had in Christianity was now entirely transferred to the East.

### The Anti-War Movement

In 1969 I began taking classes at a local university. In particular I remember a class in "Cosmology and Metaphysics." It was very disappointing. It was mainly about science and had no real cosmology, much less metaphysics. The professor was also quite disappointing. I asked him about all the world problems and what could be done to solve them. He said that humanity would be unlikely to survive another thirty-five years and there was nothing that anyone could do about it. He was content to be a professor and watch it all unfold. This caused a certain activist trend in my nature to revolt. I wanted to do something. I wasn't content to live in an intellectual ivory tower and watch the world fall apart.

Such motivation led me to the anti-war movement, though I already had an earlier interest in civil rights, which were both prominent at the time. °I became involved in the anti-war movement and participated in several anti-war protests. The movement in Colorado wasn't large and so I quickly became a visible leader and helped organize several protests. I was a member of SDS (Students for a Democratic Society) that was the largest student anti-war group and was connected to revolutionary groups of a communist and anarchist bent.

I attended SDS national conventions in Austin, Texas, and in Chicago, Illinois, in 1969. Hundreds of students gathered at these and discussed a wide variety of issues but mainly about how to start a revolution in the United States, which we all felt was a necessity. However, the SDS split in late 1969 between old socialist groups and new radical militants. The socialists wanted to appeal to the working class and tried to appear straight and conservative. I found their approach quite unappealing. At one point I considered joining the more militant groups, but was held back by my pacifistic nature. The anarchist approach most agreed with my individualistic nature, so I joined an anarchist group, but they were clearly a small minority that no one took seriously.

Along with my intellectual and political friends I started to regard the hippie movement as rather superficial, anti-intellectual and hedonistic. The fun-loving, drug-taking way of life seemed rather shallow during such a crisis of war and exploitation. I wasn't content merely seeking enjoyment but was looking for some higher goal, whether political, intellectual or spiritual.

At the same time I continued with my spiritual and philosophical studies. With my poetic and mystical background, I soon found all such political groups to be too outward in mentality. I decided that the spiritual life was better and returned to poetry and meditation as my main acitivity. I never returned to political involvement in America though I did preserve a strongly leftist, anti-bourgeoisie and anti-establishment mentality for many years, which to a great extent still remains with me.

# 3

# Spiritual Paths and Discovery of the Vedas

## Discovery of the Inner Paths

At the beginning of 1970 in Denver I found a local guru who introduced me to many spiritual teachings. While in retrospect he was limited in his insights, he did serve as a catalyst to connect me with the spiritual path. Through the encounter with various spiritual teachings that he initiated, I took to the yogic path as my main pursuit in life. He made me familiar with a broad array of mystical teachings: Hindu, Buddhist, Theosophist and Sufi. It included everything from occult teachings of Alice Bailey to Zen, and a prominent place for the teachings of Gurdjieff. I learned that a core of inner teachings existed behind the outer religious traditions of the world, an esoteric approach beyond their exoteric forms.

A number of such American teachers arose at this time, as well as teachers from India coming to the West. A major counterculture interest in India, Yoga and gurus began. The group that I was involved with was one of the few in the Denver area and so offered an alternative way of life than either my family or the counterculture, which was quite appealing at the time.

The teacher's approach was highly eclectic. He considered himself to be universal in views and would take the truth, he said, wherever he found it, which was a compelling idea. But his approach was tainted with a need to become a guru without ever having completed the disciplines that he was studying. Eventually he wrote letters to spiritual organizations all over the world asking them to become his disciples because he felt that he alone understood how to put all the different traditions together. Not surprisingly none of them took him up on his offer.

This was my first contact with spiritual hubris, which I learned was not uncommon, particularly among self-proclaimed Western gurus. The spiritual path has a strong appeal not only for the soul but also for the ego, which can gain its greatest power through it. We can become the guru and gain an uncritical adulation before we have reached our goal, which then puts an end to our search. Perhaps being exposed to spiritual egoism at a young age helped me become aware of the problem and avoid its pitfalls. I realized that spiritual practices can have side effects and even organized mystical traditions can have their excesses.

At first I found the teacher's eclectic approach to be interesting, moving on a weekly basis from one teaching or tradition to another. His approach was quite dramatic, exciting and novel, with ever-new ideas and bizarre stories. But after not long I realized such an approach was doomed to be superficial. How could one learn, much less practice all these teachings that reflected centuries of culture and the work of diverse people and which could not all be appropriate for you as an individual? While one should respect a diversity of spiritual paths, life requires choices and we must eventually follow a specific path, though hopefully one that is broad in nature.

At this time I discovered the Upanishads, in which I found great inspiration and became my favorite book. It led me to various Vedantic texts. I soon studied the works of Shankaracharya, which I avidly read in translation, particularly his shorter works like *Vivekachūḍāmaṇi*. Of the different teachings that I contacted Vedanta struck the deepest cord. I remember once climbing a hill by Denver with a friend. When we got to the top, I had the feeling that I was immortal, that the Self in me was not limited by birth and death and had lived many lives before. Such Vedantic insights seemed natural, but the friend who was with me at the time didn't understand what I was talking about.

With my philosophical bent of mind I also studied several Buddhist Sutras, especially the *Laṅkāvatāra*, which I found to be intellectually profound. The Buddhist Sutras helped serve as a bridge between the Existentialism that I had studied earlier and Eastern meditation traditions. As I encountered these teachings at a young age before my mind had become fixed, I had the benefit of an almost Eastern education to complement my Western studies.

## First Yoga Practices

My study of Eastern traditions was not merely intellectual but involved experimenting with yogic and meditational practices. I began practicing intense *prāṇāyāma*, mantra and meditation teachings in the summer of 1970. These mainly came from the Kriya Yoga tradition, which I contacted in several ways. I found that the techniques worked powerfully to create energy at a subtle level. I could feel the *prāṇa* moving through the *nāḍīs*, with some experiences of the *chakras*, and a general widening of consciousness beyond the ordinary sense of time and space. Mantra practices had a particularly powerful effect upon me. I felt that I had been some old Hindu yogi in a previous life, though in retrospect there was probably much fantasy in my approach. Another benefit from the *prāṇāyāma* was that it almost eliminated the allergies that I had suffered from for years. It cleared and cleaned my nervous system. I learned that yogic practices can heal both body and mind.

I remember walking down the streets late at night in Denver where I lived, feeling the primordial being inherent even in inanimate things – in the streets, the houses, and the plants. I could feel the spirit or Purusha enchained in matter, gradually striving to emerge through the human being. Consciousness was the basis of existence and had no boundaries. No group, idea or organization could claim it. Yet the emergence of consciousness in the human being and our body made of clay is slow, difficult and painful, though glorious in its eventual triumphs. I realized that it would be a long journey, particularly in such a materialistic culture that was asleep to all higher aspirations.

## Buddhism and Vedanta: Becoming a Vedantin

In early 1972 a friend and I moved to California to explore the spiritual groups and communities that were more common there. We visited a whole array of India groups: the Ramakrishna-Vedanta center, Self-Realization-Fellowship (SRF), an Aurobindo center, the Krishnamurti Foundation and several other gurus and their ashrams, which all taught me something. We also visited Buddhist centers, including Japanese, Chinese, Tibetan and Theravadin traditions. The direct approaches and the connection with nature in Chan and Zen were very appealing. The Tibetans with their deities and Tantric Yoga practices appeared much like Hinduism.

I felt a special affinity with Taoism and its connection with nature and found a good Chinese teacher to guide me in its study. Taoism is a religion free of dogma, close to the Earth, one with nature and not seeking converts. It was tolerant, open and non-judgmental, free of any sense of sin or moralism. I studied Taoism and the *I Ching* in some detail for several years, though more as a secondary path, which eventually led me to pursue Traditional Chinese medicine as well. I was even once ordained as a Taoist priest. However, my philosophical mind drew me more to Buddhism and Vedanta.

For a while I went back and forth between Buddhist and Vedantic perspectives. The intellectuality of Buddhism appealed to me, while the idealism of Vedanta was equally impelling. Buddhist logic had a subtlety that went beyond words and the Buddhist understanding of the mind had a depth that was extraordinary, dwarfing that of Western Psychology. But Vedanta had a sense of Pure Being and Consciousness that was more in harmony with my deeper mystical urges. It reflected the soul and its perennial aspiration for the Divine that seemed obvious to me.

I felt the need of a cosmic creator such as Buddhism did not have. It was not the old monotheistic tyrant with his heaven and hell, but the wise and loving Divine Father and Mother, such as in the Hindu figures of Shiva and Pārvati. I also found the existence of the Atman or higher Self to be self-evident. That all is the Self appeared to be the most self-evident truth of existence. The Buddhist non-ego approach made sense as a rejection of the lower or false Self but I saw no need to dismiss the Self altogether as many Buddhists do.

I couldn't understand why Buddhism, which after all arose in India, rejected Atman, Brahman or Ishvara, or why they couldn't accept the Upanishads as valid or complete teachings. Besides the Vedantic view was quite open and not dogmatic. It seemed that Buddhism had taken certain Vedantic ideas and reformulated them, turning Brahman into the Dharmakāya, Atman into Bodhichitta, and God or Ishvara into Buddha. So, however much I admired Buddhism, I saw no need to become a Buddhist apart from Vedanta. The result was that I became a Vedantin and accepted it as my life's philosophy, which has remained so ever since. I found it easy to integrate Buddhist insights into this Vedantic mold.

This shift from a general exploration of the world's different spiritual paths to a specific following of Vedanta was another important stage in my development. I no longer tried to study everything, much less felt that I had to practice everything.

**Ramana Maharshi, the Ultimate Sage**

At first it seemed that Vedanta did not have quite the intellectual sophistication of Buddhism and its direct mind teachings. Then I discovered Advaita Vedanta texts like *Avadhūta Gītā* and *Ashṭāvakra Saṁhitā* that had this as well. But more importantly I learned of a teacher who had the most enlightened teaching that I had seen anywhere.

In the teachings of the Advaitic sage Ramana Maharshi I discovered a Vedanta that was alive and intellectually sophisticated, yet spiritually profound and experiential. Ramana Maharshi was like the quintessential sage, who perfectly understood all the workings of the mind as well as the consciousness beyond it. I felt an immediate pull from his picture from my first encounter with it. Ramana has remained as a kind of spiritual father and as the ultimate model for enlightenment. I also corresponded with his ashram in India and studied their magazine, the *Mountain Path,* which I would later write articles for.

Self-knowledge is the essence of all spiritual paths and the basis of Vedanta, whose main motto is Know Thyself. Ramana embodied this path of Self-knowledge completely and lived it fully. With him Vedanta became a living presence, a radiant flame that persisted throughout all time and space. At the same time Ramana was not trapped in tradition or ceremony, mere book learning or dry ritual. His Advaita was simple, direct and modern, as well as faithful to the highest realization. It was quite adaptable and open to each individual. I felt perfectly at home with it.

Ramana's influence combined with that of the Ramakrishna order, the Upanishads and Shankaracharya became the basis of my Vedantic path. I also studied other important Advaitic texts and tried to develop an informed view of the tradition. In terms of my practices I switched to Jñāna Yoga, the Yoga of knowledge or Self-inquiry approach, such as taught by Ramana, with some influence of J. Krishnamurti. Such meditation approaches were both calming and deepening. Though I examined the main yoga teachers and spiritual groups in the West, I didn't find a teacher among them that I could specifically follow. With my individualistic nature I avoided the more popular and faddish movements. But I did develop a strong sense of commitment to tradition.

## Sufism

In my examination of the world's spiritual traditions I looked into Sufism, starting through the teachings of Gurdjieff, who had major connections with them. My initial impression was that the Sufis had a high level mystical tradition, equal to those of the Hindus and Buddhists, and more sophisticated than the Christian mystics. The Sufis spoke of self-knowledge and self-realization and the unity of all religions.

However, I soon noticed an intolerance and regimentation among the Sufis that became progressively disturbing to me. Claims that the Sufis created Advaita Vedanta in India or were responsible for Zen in Japan seemed quite exaggerated. The Sufis emphasized a kind of conformity or group work that did not appeal to my individualistic nature. They also used Biblical terms that reminded me of Christianity and its dogma. Their God seemed too personal and too emotional. I preferred the more detached and impersonal pure consciousness of dharmic traditions.

I had occasional contacts with various Sufis through the years. I visited several of their centers and spoke with them on many topics. Many American born Sufis viewed Sufism in a yogic way. Their connection is more to Rumi than to Mohammed. But the Sufis that I met who had strong overseas connections were different. They saw Islam as better than the dharmic traditions of the East and insisted that one become an orthodox Muslim before becoming a Sufi. This caused me to lose interest in the Sufi path.

## Discovery of the Vedas/Sri Aurobindo

Among the spiritual teachers whose writings I studied, most notable in terms of my own thought and expression, was Sri Aurobindo. Aurobindo possessed an intellectual breadth that was unparalleled by any author I had ever read. One could swim in the field of his mind like a whale in the open sea and never encounter any limits. He dwarfed the Western intellectuals that I studied and even the Western mystics. Relative to Indian teachers, his teaching was clear, modern, liberal and poetic, not tainted by caste, authority or dogma. Aurobindo's vision encompassed the past, revealing the mysteries of the ancient world that I had long sought. But it showed the way to the future as well, with a balanced and universal vision of humanity for all time.

Aurobindo synthesized the great traditions of India and transformed them into something of global relevance, pioneering a New Age of consciousness. He clearly understood Western culture, both its intellectual heights and its spiritual limitations. He could reflect what was valuable in Western literature and philosophy, while also being a devastating critic of the Western mind and its attachment to outer forms and material realities.

I studied a number of Aurobindo's works, notably the *Life Divine,* which unraveled all the secrets of the philosophies of India from Vedanta to Sāmkhya, Yoga and Tantra. In it I noted the various verses from the *Rigveda* that he used to open the chapters. I found these to be quite profound and mysterious and wanted to learn more of the Vedas. In looking through the titles of Sri Aurobindo a book called *Hymns to the Mystic Fire,* which was hymns to Agni from the *Rigveda,* struck a cord with my poetic vision. It led me to another book *Secret of the Veda,* which more specifically explained the Vedic teaching and opened up the Vedic vision for me.

*Secret of the Veda* became a key work in my life, which I read many times. I remember one particular instance in which I was taking a bus from Colorado to Canada where I was visiting friends, reading the book late at night. It must have been Spring of 1971. A Vedic epiphany dawned on me. I could sense the march of Vedic dawns unfolding a continual evolution of consciousness in the universe. I could feel the Vedic wisdom permeating all of nature, unfolding the secrets of birth and death, the days and nights of the soul. The Veda was present at the core of our being like an inextinguishable flame and carried the spiritual aspiration of our species. It was sad to contemplate how far we had fallen – that culturally we had closed the doors on these ancient dawns and become mired in a dark night of greed and arrogance.

At that time I became a Vedic person, not simply a Vedantin. While becoming a Vedantin was the first level of my inner change, becoming Vedic was the second stage. These two transitions overlapped to a great degree. I followed the Vedas in the context of Vedanta. But later a more specific Vedic vision emerged and came to dominate over the Vedantic view. It brought a wider and more integral Vedanta and one that connected with poetry and mantra.

After a more thorough study of Vedanta I soon learned that few Vedantins study the Vedas or see in them the depth of wisdom that Aurobindo did and which seemed so natural to me. Becoming a Vedic person took me to another place than most Vedantins, who mainly reject the Vedas as only of ritualistic value. I saw the Vedas as adding a symbolic or mantric level of knowledge to Vedanta. Eventually this dimension of Vedic mantras became more interesting than Vedantic logic or inquiry. It was like entering into another time, another state of mind, a different language and a different humanity. The philosophical side of my mind gradually receded in favor of a Vedic mantric approach.

I had to break through my attachment to the sophisticated philosophical dialectic of Vedanta and Buddhism in order to appreciate the primeval images of the older Vedas. This was perhaps as difficult and radical a change as moving from a Western intellectual view to that of yogic spirituality. It was also one in which I found myself even more alone. While a number of people I knew followed Yogic and Vedantic paths, for many years I had no real friends who shared such a connection with the Vedas.

I held this Vedic vision for several years but did not really immerse myself into it until 1978, though I continued to study Vedic and Vedantic teachings in the meantime. Sometimes I tried to go back from the Vedic vision to a more Vedantic logic, just as previously I had gone back and forth from Vedantic views to Western artistic and intellectual ideas. My transition to a full Vedic view took its own time. Sri Aurobindo's work also helped me develop my own poetic vision which aided in this transition.

**Anandamayi Ma**

From 1976 through 1980 I corresponded with the great woman saint of India, Sri Anandamayi Ma. I had decided to write her as a friend of mine had recently done so and received a reply. To my surprise a letter came back from her within a few months. Swamis Atmananda and Nirvanananda helped with my communications.

I planned to visit Ma in India but somehow could not get the resources together to bring it about. I also wrote a few articles for their magazine *Ananda Varta*. Contact with Ma inspired me more into a Vedantic and Hindu mold. Her energy would come in waves, almost like an electrical force, encouraging me to deeper practices. Ma's energy opened up devotional potentials for me, not merely for the Goddess but also for Shiva and Rama. I began to look into Bhakti Yoga, chanting and devotional meditation. Images of Hindu deities appeared in my mind.

Under Ma's inspiration I began a more serious study of Vedic teachings. About this time I also received a copy of the *Yajurveda* from India, which I found, to my surprise since even Aurobindo hadn't talked of it, to be as inspiring as the *Rigveda*. The power of the mantras continued to unfold and new Vedic vistas arose.

About the same time I discovered the teachings of Swami Rama Tirtha, who lived at the turn of the century and was another great Vedantin. I felt a special inner kinship to Swami Rama, who was a poetic, inspirational and independent figure. I felt that Ma's grace led me to him, as the Ram mantra often came to me while I was in contact with her. Swami Rama was another major guide and teacher in my life. Most importantly he connected me with the world of nature through his towering Himalayan spirit and his indomitable will.

## Writing on the Vedas

Then in summer of 1978 my Vedic work, which would dominate the rest of my life, first emerged. I was inspired by some inner energy to write a set of poems about the ancient dawns and the ancient suns that directed me back to the Vedas. I decided to study the Vedas in depth in the original Sanskrit. I wanted to directly confirm if Sri Aurobindo's view was correct that the Vedas did have a deeper spiritual and Vedantic meaning. I had studied Sanskrit through the years and already had Sanskrit texts of the Vedas and Upanishads to start with.

I remember my early encounters with Vedic texts. Sometimes they seemed primitive or even violent in their language. I thought that either the Vedic Rishis were not true sages or that something was fundamentally wrong in how we have interpreted their teachings. Rather than simply dismissing the Vedas as primitive I decided to question the perspective. I found that most people were looking at the Vedas through the eyes of Western intellectual thought or, at best, with a Vedantic or Buddhist logic. I realized that the Vedas were not written according to either of these views and required a very different approach.

It is not enough merely to translate the Vedas; one has to recreate the background the Vedas came from, in which context they were fresh and alive. The Vedas presumed a certain state of mind on the part of those who studied them. Like a treatise on high energy physics that requires a knowledge of elementary physics to approach, the Vedas were designed for people who already had a sense of the Vedic language and its implications. Without recreating that Vedic background merely to translate the Vedas only invites misinterpretation. I decided to try to recreate that background. The result was that I discovered deeper meaning to teachings that appeared as little more than primitive rituals to others.

Because of my background in poetic symbolism the Vedas made perfect sense to me. The Sun, day, dawn, fire, and ocean were archetypes of inner processes. So were such animal images as the bull, cow, horse or falcon. I didn't view Vedic images according to the standard of Vedantic or Buddhist logic, looking for some subtle abstract dialectic, from which angle they would appear crude. I saw them as analogical keys to the workings of the universe. I began creating a system to unlock the greater meaning of the Vedic language.

I developed a strategy. I decided that the best way to proceed was to trace the Vedic vision back from the Upanishads, which were still relatively transparent in meaning, to the Vedas – to use the Upanishads as a door back in time. Most people started the Hindu tradition with the Upanishads and took them as its foundation. They saw the emergence of the exalted philosophy of Vedanta in the Upanishads and took that as the essence of the tradition. Following Aurobindo I realized that the Upanishads were a transitional literature. While they created the basis for what came later, they also reflected the essence of what was done earlier. While they opened the door forward on the classical Hindu-Buddhist world, they closed the door backward on the more mysterious Vedic age. I began intensely working on the early Upanishads, in what eventually became my first published book in India, the *Creative Vision of the Early Upanishads*.

I correlated various Upanishadic passages that either quoted from the earlier Vedas or paraphrased them. I found that many Upanishadic verses came directly from the earlier Vedas, which most translators and commentators didn't seem to know. The same verse occurring in the Upanishads would be given a spiritual meaning, while in the Vedas it was taken as merely ritualistic, if not primitive! I used this Upanishadic usage of Vedic verses to give an Upanishadic meaning to the Vedic hymns. I felt that if the Upanishads could use Vedic type verses for expressing Self-realization, all the verses of the Vedas should have a similar potential.

I took the very portions of the early Upanishads usually rejected as ritualistic and reinterpreted them from a spiritual angle, in light of the rules of symbolic language. I was particularly affected by the *Chāndogya Upanishad*, which comes from the *Sāmaveda* or the Veda of song. The book itself would seem to sing or to chant to me. I would merely look at the book and start to hear the Vedic students of old raising their voices to the Divine. Something of the Vedic *shakti* came through it along with a connection to the ancient seers, their families and their practices.

I learned to look back from Advaita Vedanta through the Upanishads into the mantras of the *Rigveda*, seeing how the path of Self-realization was there in the earliest hymns. Like Aurobindo I could appreciate the Vedic mantras as a pure spiritual experience that later became reduced to mere ritual when the inner meaning of the symbols was forgotten. The Vedic mantras also served to open the entire ancient spiritual world for me, affording a sense of the deeper meaning of Egyptian or Mayan symbols as well.

The Vedic language came alive and showed its meaning to me. I found a Vedantic or *ādhyātmika* vision in nearly all the Vedic mantras, but most Vedantins do not see this.

Shankaracharya, the great Vedantic commentator, did not make Vedantic comments on the Vedic mantras but only on the Upanishads, and only on small portions of the early Upanishads. He divided the Vedas into the Karma Kāṇḍa or section of works and the Jñāna Kāṇḍa or section of knowledge. He placed the Vedic mantras and Brahmanas in the former section and only the Upanishads in the latter. This to me was like consigning all the Vedas except the Upanishads to the domain of mere ritual, which was effectively to dismiss the bulk of Vedic literature, not to connect with their great power and legacy.

This Vedantic dismissing of the Vedas gave the impression that the Vedic Rishis did not have the knowledge or the realization of the Upanishadic sages. This was odd because the Upanishadic sages quoted the Vedic Rishis to support their knowledge. I looked at the matter differently. Like Aurobindo I felt that there was a way of Self-realization in the *Rigveda*. Shankara's division of the Vedas into Jñāna Kāṇḍa and Karma Kāṇḍa was a matter of convenience and not the last word. He spoke to an audience that was unable to see the deeper meaning of the Vedic mantras but could understand the logic of Vedanta. The more accurate view is that the Vedas contain both knowledge and ritual and the Vedic mantras can be interpreted in either sense. The Brahmanas are mainly ritualistic, while the Upanishads emphasize knowledge, but the Saṁhitā or mantra portion of the Vedas can be looked at in either sense.

## M.P. Pandit

After finishing this Vedic study I had no idea what to do with it. Fortunately, through a personal friend I came into contact with M.P. Pandit, the secretary of the Sri Aurobindo Ashram. I had long admired Pandit's many books on the Vedas, Tantra, Sri Aurobindo and the Mother. Pandit was perhaps the foremost scholar of Indian spirituality, not from an academic view but from a real understanding and inner experience that spanned the entire tradition. If anyone could appreciate what I was doing, it was he.

I first visited Pandit in San Francisco in the summer of 1979. I brought my writings on the Vedas and Upanishads and explained my approach to him. What I received from him in return went far beyond my expectations. Pandit was a calm and concentrated person, with a penetrating vision. He listened carefully before making any comments. Instead of trying to influence me he was quite receptive and open to what I was attempting. I told him that I was not an academic but doing the work from an inner motivation and an intuitive view. He said that it was better that I was not an academic because I would not repeat their same old mistakes and could gain a fresh view of the subject!

Pandit strongly encouraged me to continue my work, offering his full support. He called my Vedic work my "Divine mission," that I should follow out. He said both to my surprise and my honor that he would get my writings published in India. This greatly increased my enthusiasm in what I was doing, which up to that point appeared to be some obscure personal study, perhaps relevant to no one. He asked me to mail him some of my writings in India as he would be returning to India in a few months.

Over the next few months I wrote a new book on the *Rigveda* called *Self-realization and the Supermind in the Rigveda* and sent it to him. The manuscript was over five hundred pages long and consisted of translations and interpretations of many different Sūktas, particularly those to Indra. I had worked on it day and night during that period. He serialized the book first in *World Union* and later in the *Advent,* major Sri Aurobindo Ashram journals from 1980-1984. Later I sent Pandit various chapters of the *Shukla Yajurveda,* which I similarly translated and interpreted in a spiritual (*ādhyātmika*) light. This he had serialized in *Sri Aurobindo's Action.* Pandit also got my book *Creative Vision of the Early Upanishads* published in India. His help was crucial in establishing my work as a writer in the Vedic field, without which it would have been probably consigned to my desk!

Along with Pandit came the additional gift of the grace of the Mother of the Sri Aurobindo Ashram. After contacting Pandit I could also feel the Mother's energy and presence around me. She was close by and would quickly appear to my inner vision, guiding me in various ways. Even today I can feel her nearby my consciousness whenever I think of her. This was not something I cultivated but came of its own accord.

## J. Krishnamurti and the Question of Tradition

Another important, but rather opposite spiritual influence, at the time was J. Krishnamurti. In California I happened to end up for a few years at Ojai, the town where Krishnamurti gave his yearly talks, which I attended regularly. I became familiar with the Krishnamurti community and made friends with several older members of the group, most who were ex-Theosophists. Krishnamurti's thoughts had a logic that appealed to my revolutionary and anti-authority mentality. He was a kind of spiritual anarchist. Though he was in favor of meditation and the spiritual life, he was against gurus and structured practices. Yet given my connections with the Vedas and Vedanta I couldn't accept his wholesale rejection of tradition and technique, or his criticism of mantra.

Krishnamurti was, on one hand, a typically self-alienated Indian intellectual criticizing his own culture. But, on the other hand, he possessed a genuine meditative mind in harmony with the same tradition, a strange contradiction but one that was appealing to people who could not relate to traditions. He had important teachings on perception and on the workings of the mind and emotions that added much depth to my meditation.

Krishnamurti wanted to create a teaching that was universal, that was not culturally limited or conditioned, and did not require any identity in order to follow. While this was a noble endeavor it failed to note the organic nature of life. In refusing to align with any tradition his teaching became limited to perhaps the most limited factor. It became a one man teaching or one-man tradition – a Krishnamurti teaching.

All tradition is not bad. Otherwise we should leave our infants in the woods and let them raise themselves without authority, tradition or interference. We all follow various traditions in life. We are part of a society and a collective evolution. We as individuals don't invent our own language, much less our own spiritual teachings. We have to take the good that the collective culture gives us and carry it further along.

An authoritarian tradition that does not allow open questioning but projects a dogma as truth is certainly harmful. But a cultural tradition that promotes spirituality and creativity is very helpful. For example, a musical tradition provides the instruments and tools for musicians to grow. Spiritual traditions can be helpful springboards for self-realization. The problem arises when their tools are applied mechanically, which is unfortunately too often the case. Real knowledge has a tradition and an authority, just as there is in science, but it is a matter of direct experience, not of mere belief. This is the basis of the real Vedic tradition.

One important thing I did learn from Krishnamurti was not to blindly follow anyone who called himself a guru. Later I learned that it is particularly dangerous to follow a guru who does not represent or have the sanction of any real tradition. The Vedic view allows thinking and debate and can even accept a Krishnamurti who rejects the tradition for his insights on meditation.

## Into the Vedic Work – Ayurveda and Vedic Astrology

Ayurveda became my main vehicle for expressing Vedic knowledge to a modern and Western audience. This also occurred according to a certain chance or synchronicity. I moved to Santa Fe, New Mexico, in early 1983, where I focused on the study of herbs and natural medicine that I had already been engaged in for some time as part of my seeking for a dharmic livelihood. The alternative medicine movement was beginning in a big way. But I didn't know that an Indian Ayurvedic doctor was then teaching the first Ayurvedic programs in the United States in Santa Fe. I was introduced to him by chance. His school was interested in having someone teach Sanskrit, a role that I found out about and took up. In turn I began an intense study of Ayurveda. This led to my teaching and writing in the field and helping create study programs and classes.

Along a parallel line I had taken up the study of Vedic Astrology. I first studied Astrology in Ojai in the early seventies, which with a Theosophical center had good resources on the subject. I also discovered a few good books on Vedic Astrology. I practiced Western Astrology for several years, using Vedic Astrology as a sidelight, but gradually shifted over to the Vedic system. Along with my Ayurvedic work in the mid-eighties I focused on Vedic Astrology, introducing classes and courses in it as well, starting with Ayurveda students.

In such diverse endeavors I wasn't following a particular plan but simply pursuing my interests that often seemed scattered or disconnected. Several times I tried to reduce one or more areas of involvement so as to concentrate my energies, but circumstances kept me active in all these different fields. Later I would discover that the Vedic vision could integrate such disparate subjects and was behind my involvement with all of them.

With Ayurveda and Vedic Astrology I discovered a practical usage of Vedic knowledge that was relevant to everyone. The gap between my Vedic work and my actual career began to disappear. My Vedic work and my livelihood became interrelated. I focused on Ayurveda and Vedic Astrology for a few years and put my Vedic pursuits temporarily in the background.

# 4

# India and Hinduism

I had studied Hindu teachings and corresponded with ashrams and teachers in India for many years. I had written articles for journals in India since 1978 and books from 1982. But I hadn't actually been to India, though I almost made it twice. One of my Hindu teachers in America remarked, "David didn't go to India, India came to him."

In 1987 I traveled to China and Tibet as part of my study of Chinese medicine. A few months later, I took a second trip to Asia and finally made it to India. Though, perhaps belatedly, visiting India was an important and transformative experience, marking another era in my life. After that first visit I continued to go back to India on a yearly basis.

My first trip to India occurred as part of my pursuit of Ayurveda. It involved visiting Ayurvedic schools and companies in Bombay and Nagpur, and sightseeing to other parts of the country. I also had two important visits of a spiritual nature, first to Pondicherry and the Sri Aurobindo Ashram, and second to the Ramanashram in nearby Tiruvannamalai, a pattern that was repeated in future visits to the country.

## Sri Aurobindo and Pondicherry

My visit to Pondicherry and the Sri Aurobindo Ashram reconnected me with Sri Aurobindo and the Mother. There is definitely a strong *shakti* present in the town, the Mother's force that is almost palpable. It came over me like a wave and took me out of my ordinary consciousness, sometimes for hours on end. It literally flattened me, putting me in a state in which I didn't want to move. Sri Aurobindo's force was also there, particularly at his *samādhi* shrine, in which I could feel and experience his life and teachings. But the Mother's *shakti* permeated the entire city and never left one.

Pondicherry provided the opportunity to visit with M.P. Pandit, who I had not seen since he stopped coming to the West a few years earlier. I had kept in touch with him by correspondence and he had reviewed my various books that had come out in the meantime.

One day I was attending one of Pandit's weekly meditations that followed his weekly talks. Suddenly I started to breathe deeply and felt my consciousness open up to a higher plane. The vision of the Mother of the ashram unfolded as the White Goddess Tara, a figure of great beauty, light and compassion. Tibetan monks were doing chants to her and seeking to project her energy in order to help save the human race from the ignorance and illusion in which it was mired. They were meditating upon suffering humanity and using the Mother's force to uplift people.

The history of humanity unfolded before my inner eye, how as children of Manu or the mind, we have an inherent ignorance that keeps us trapped in duality and sorrow. This ignorance at the core of our minds has become the matrix of our culture which, therefore, is caught in dichotomy, contradiction and disintegration. Until we move beyond this limited mental consciousness we must repeat the same old errors and live in the same uncertainty.

Yet beyond all this suffering the Mother revealed a new and higher plan of creation, a model for a new human being beyond the old mortal conditioning of lust, fear and hatred. This being lived in harmony with nature in an almost paradise situation but as a future potential, not as a fact of the Earth life, which would require much time and effort to manifest it. The Mother kept echoing the need for a new creation for which she was projecting the seeds and scattering the flowers all over the world.

I gradually returned to the ordinary state of consciousness as the meditation came to an end. As I left the house Pandit offered me a flower, a white jasmine dear to the Mother, as said "for a new creation." While I have done much work with the ancient Vedas it is not only for the past, but also for the future – going back to the human origins in order to create a new humanity in harmony with the Divine dawns and embodying the Divine light.

## The Ramanashram: Encounter with Lord Skanda

Ramana Maharshi is probably the most famous enlightened sage of modern India, the very personification of the Atman, a pure unbounded Self-realization, even though he did nothing to gain recognition for himself. He has great appeal to a rational and modern mind willing to transcend name, form and culture. Yet what I discovered at his ashram and in the psychic environment of the town and hill was something different and unexpected.

I came to the Ramanashram to contact Ramana and his path of Self-inquiry, which is a method to experience the non-dual state of pure awareness. What I actually discovered was the God Skanda, the child of fire, who demanded purification, death and spiritual rebirth. I encountered one of the Gods, not as a devotional or cultural image but as a primordial and awesome power. Ramana came to me through Lord Skanda, the son of Shiva, with whom Ganapati Muni identified him. I came to understand Ramana as Lord Skanda, the embodiment of the flame of knowledge.

Coming into Tiruvannamalai I felt the presence of a tremendous spiritual fire, which also had, in its more benefic moments, the face of a young boy. The image of a small boy carrying a spear, rising out of a fire, kept arising in my mind. This brought about an intense practice of Self-inquiry that was literally like death, though it was the ego's death, not that of the body. Going through that fire was perhaps the most intense spiritual experience of my life, to the point that I had at time to pray that it would not become too strong! Yet afterwards I felt refreshed and cleansed, with a purity of perception that was extraordinary.

Up to that point I had a limited understanding of the role of deities in spiritual practice. I had almost no knowledge of Lord Skanda, though he is a popular deity in South India and one sees his picture everywhere. I had not yet grasped the depth of his connection with Ramana. So I was shocked to come into a direct contact with such an entity, not as a mere fantasy but as a concrete and vivid inner experience penetrating to the core of my being. That the process of Self-inquiry, which starts out as a philosophical practice, could be aligned to a deity in which my personality was swallowed up, was not something that I had noted in any teachings.

In time I learned much about both Skanda and Ramana. Skanda is the incarnation of the power of direct insight. He is the Self that is born of Self-inquiry which is like a fire, the inner child born of the death of the ego on the cremation pyre of meditation. This child represents the innocent mind, free of ulterior motives, which alone can destroy all the demons, our negative conditionings, with his spear of discrimination beyond the fluctuations of the mind. Coming to Tiruvannamalai was an experience of that inner fire (*tejas*) which is Skanda and Ramana.

I felt Lord Skanda most keenly at the great temple of Arunachaleshwara in the nearby town. Initially the experience of the temple was more important for me than the experience of the ashram. Arunachaleshwara temple still holds the vibration of Ramana, who was its child, where he stayed and practiced *tapas* when young and unknown. The temple has its own Divine presence that has nourished many great sages and yogis.

The Devi (Goddess) at the temple functions as the mother of Ramana and Skanda and the mother of all true seekers. The great Shiva linga, similarly, is like Ramana's father. The deities in the temple came alive as the parents of Lord

Skanda, who was not only Ramana, but also my own inner child of immortality. I felt the strongest energy and unfoldment in the Mother temple. The story of the birth of the Goddess Uma, her *tapas* in the Himalayas, her marriage with Lord Shiva, and the birth of Lord Skanda began to unfold in my meditations as a symbol of the process of Self-realization. The myth became real, while our human lives became mere shadows. The realms of these deities (*Devalokas*) emerged as states of meditation or planes of awareness.

One day at the temple I decided to purchase a statue to take back home for my altar. I found a small statue of Lord Skanda that I bought and put into my nap sack. One of the Brahmin priests in the temple noted my acquisition and asked for the statue, which I gave to him. He took my hand and led me through the temple, doing the puja to the main deities. He started with the Devi temple and then to the Shiva linga and finally to the Skanda temple. My statue was placed on all these *mūrtis* and was consecrated as part of the pujas. It was as if I myself was reborn as Skanda during these rites.

## The Goddess

The figure of the Goddess appeared strong in my poetry since a child, but it was in India that I came to really experience her, first at the Tiruvannamalai temple and at the Ramanashram, but later at many places in the country. I have always felt myself to be a child of the Goddess.

Once while I was meditating at the ashram the Devi appeared to me in a form of Durga called Mahishāsuramardinī holding various ornaments and weapons. She offered these to me and placed them in my mind. I was puzzled at first and wondered what I was supposed to do with them. I later came to know that they were some of the different teachings and practices that she bestowed on her devotees. I remember feeling them in my mind when I was on the plane to the USA as if all the Gods and Goddesses were riding back with me.

One needs many tools in order to be successful in one's spiritual work. Many obstacles lie along the way, which

require different methods to overcome. These divine
weapons help us break through them. The divine ornaments
give beauty to charm difficulties away. Such tools proved
helpful, if not crucial through time. Rather than struggling
with problems, I call upon the weapons of the Goddess to
deal with them.

I later realized that Durga was the form of the Goddess
connected with Bharat Mata or Mother India, who took the
form of Durga riding her lion. Later I came to understand that
her blessing was a presage of my later journalistic work in the
country, which I had no idea about at the time. The weapons
and ornaments were mantric tools to do this work.

It was if I had become one of the Divine Mother's warriors.
These I first experienced in the form of the Vedic Maruts or
Wind Gods, the sons of Rudra-Shiva and the companions of
Indra. Later I would realize their connection with the deity
Hanuman who is also the son of the Wind God and the head
of the divine army. I joined the Mother Durga's army, though
not knowingly at first.

## Sadhu on the Hill

One day during one of my several trips to the ashram I
decided to climb the great hill of Arunachala. It is a moderate
hike of about two hours. That particular day was a little
cloudy so the heat was not unbearable. After I reached the
top of the hill I stopped to meditate for a few minutes. There
one finds the remains of the fires, the bricks and pottery,
which are burned yearly on the full moon of the month of
Kārttika, which is sacred to Lord Skanda.

While sitting by these I suddenly saw an old figure dressed
in orange taking very wide strides and coming up the hill. He
stopped in a few places and picked a few berries from the
sparse vegetation. Then he came to within about fifty feet
and looked at me, giving the *siddha* gesture with his hand. At
that instant the whole of space opened up behind me. I could
feel the infinite void extending in all directions and my entire
life felt like a bubble within it. It was like a moment out of

time. Then he continued with his wide strides and went to the other side of the hill and disappeared.

I am not certain who the sadhu was. He did not look like Ramana but more like an old wandering Swami. Ramana said that Siddhas dwelled on the hill. I could say from my experience that this was the case. India still has such mysterious figures that one can contact, sense or intuit at times. That is part of the blessing of visiting the land.

## Ganapati Muni and Sri Natesan

My mind had been in a curious dilemma for several years. On one hand, I had a strong connection with Ramana Maharshi. On the other hand, I had an equally strong connection with Sri Aurobindo whose teaching was very different. Though I held Ramana as the ideal, my own work and writings made more sense in terms of Sri Aurobindo's teaching.

This dilemma began to resolve itself in an unexpected way. I studied the works of Kapali Shastri, the guru of M.P. Pandit, who wrote extensively on the Vedas from Sri Aurobindo's point of view. Many of my comments on the Upanishads that I had written were echoed in Kapali's work. I eventually discovered that Kapali, prior to connecting with Aurobindo had been a disciple of Ramana Maharshi. He was responsible for many of the Sanskrit works on Ramana under the pseudonym K.

Kapali was the chief disciple of Ganapati Muni, who was perhaps the chief disciple of Ramana. Ganapati had first discovered Ramana as a young boy then called Brahma Swami, because he was a Brahmin boy. He renamed him Ramana and Bhagavan. Ganapati wrote several important Sanskrit works on the Maharshi and also put Ramana's teachings into Sanskrit, which Kapali as his disciple commented on.

I decided to search out the works of Ganapati Muni, particularly on the Vedas, as he was reputed to be a Vedic scholar as well. I asked M.P. Pandit about Ganapati and whether his Vedic work was important. He said that there was little about the Vedas in the scattered works of Ganapati, though Ganapati did accept an exalted status for the Vedic mantras. I asked at the Ramanashram about Ganapati and his Vedic works but at first nothing came of it.

In 1992, I came in contact with K. Natesan, who in his eighties, was one of the oldest living disciples of Ganapati and Ramana. When Natesan discovered my interest in Ganapati he revealed his great secret. He had collected Ganapati's work for decades. Besides copies of Ganapati's printed works, most of which were out of print, he had painstakingly transcribed Ganapati's handwritten manuscripts and gathered nearly all of them. He had much material that even M.P. Pandit never knew about, including extensive works on the Vedas by Ganapati. He happily made copies of all these works for me and I took them back home to America to study. Natesan guided me to Ganapati and became a source of his grace and his influence.

In Ganapati's works I found an approach to the Vedas in harmony with my deepest thoughts. The emphasis on Indra that I had already developed in my writings was also there in his Thousand Names of Indra. He understood Agni as Skanda and as Ramana, which made perfect sense to me. I also began to come into contact with Ganapati on a subtle level, feeling an inner rapport and transmission of knowledge. It was as if he was speaking to me in my own mind.

Ganapati was a Vedic scholar, a Tantric yogi, an Ayurvedic doctor and a Vedic astrologer, as well as an active social thinker and reformer – covering the same basic range of fields that I had and at a much deeper level. He even researched the history of the Vedas and the *Mahābhārata*. He was probably the greatest Sanskrit poet and writer of this century. His greatest work, *Umā Sahasram*, has a thousand verses and forty chapters each down flawlessly in a different Sanskrit meter. I recognized him as a model for what I was attempting in all aspects of my work. He also presented an approach that balanced my connection with both Aurobindo and Ramana. Through Ganapati I was able to bridge the gap between the two. No doubt a secret affinity with him was behind the position that I had taken.

Natesan has remained as an important friend and mentor, helping me on several levels inwardly and outwardly. He has continued to pass on special teachings over the years, not only from Ganapati but also from Ramana and from Sri Aurobindo, as he remains in contact with both ashrams. Ganapati came to me through Natesan and became a personal example for me to follow. He shared my same varied interests and integrated them as part of his greater spiritual path.

## The Goddesses and Bhakti Yoga

Ganapati's work contained an extensive teaching on the *Daśa Mahāvidyā* or ten great knowledge forms of the Goddesses. I wrote about this subject in my book *Tantric Yoga and the Wisdom Goddesses*, using Ganapati's teachings. Ganapati was also closely connected to Uma, Renuka, Chinnamasta and many other forms of the Goddess. His teachings took me deeper into Devi worship. Using various Goddess mantras has been central to my yogic practice. Most of these mantras have come from Ganapati and Natesan. Mantra after all is the form of the Goddess.

Bhakti Yoga became progressively more important for me. Its value can be described with a simple metaphor: knowledge (*jñāna*) is the flame and the mind is the wick, but *bhakti* is the oil. Without *bhakti* spiritual knowledge burns out the mind, like a flame does a wick without oil.

I discovered that the Vedas are primarily books on Bhakti Yoga, quite contrary to a modern scholarly belief that Bhakti Yoga originated from a later Islamic or Christian influence in medieval India. The Vedas worship the Divine in all the forms of nature including human (Gods like Indra), animal (vehicles of the gods like the bull and the horse), plant (the sacred *aśvattha* tree and Soma plant), elemental (like fire and water), and cosmic (like the sun). They explain all attitudes of devotion honoring the Divine as the father, mother, brother, sister, friend, son, daughter, child and master. The whole Vedic concept of *namas* or surrender to the Gods is itself the essence of *bhakti*. The *Rigveda* also frequently mentions the sacred or secret Divine Names, showing that chanting the names of God and meditation upon them was always central to the Vedic path.

This stream of *bhakti* has kept Hinduism alive and flowering throughout the ages from the *Rigveda* to the *Mahābhārata* and the Puranas, from the Alvars and Nayanars in the south to Tulsidas and Mirabai in the north of the country. *Bhakti* is the real heart of Hinduism. It is a Divine love founded not on dogma or sin but on the very exuberance of life itself, which is ever seeking transcendence and greater awareness. From baby Krishna, to Rama with his bow, to Durga on her lion it has touched all the themes of life with great feeling, personal intimacy and poignancy.

I learned to chant various stotras to the Gods and Goddesses, particularly those of Shankaracharya, who produced many wonderful ones, which became a regular practice for me. J. Jayaraman, the librarian at the Ramanashram and both a great sadhu and musician aided me in this pursuit. Without dipping into the waters of devotion, I find that my intellectual work is not fulfilling. Often I spend my evenings in devotional practices after days of more mental work. This devotion is mainly to the Goddess but includes the whole range of Vedic and Hindu deities, including Indra, Agni, Shiva, Rama, Hanuman and Ganesha.

## Brahmarshi Daivarata

A few years later while giving a talk at the Bharatiya Vidya Bhavan in Mumbai I was given a curious present, a book called *Chandodarśana* by Daivarata, another important disciple of Ganapati Muni and Ramana Maharshi. The Bhavan members didn't know of my connection with Ganapati, so it was a coincidence. I later received *Vāksudhā,* another work of Daivarata as well.

Daivarata followed Ganapati's vision but unlike Kapali remained close to Ramana and did not join Aurobindo. He developed a Vedic view based upon Ganapati's ideas, including his own direct vision of new Vedic mantras much like the rishis of old. He also worshipped the Goddess, particularly as Sarasvati and Tara. I learned later that Maharishi Mahesh Yogi brought Daivarata to the West in the early seventies as a living example of a modern Vedic Rishi with the full knowledge of the Vedas and the power of its mantras. I found great inspiration in his work. Daivarata like Ganapati entered into my psyche as a key part of the new Vedic renaissance.

## The Himalayas

Hinduism is the spirit of the Himalayas. It is a vision fostered by these lofty subtropical mountains and their abundant rivers that combine both height and depth, both austerity and abundance.

Haridwar at the doorway to the Himalayas is the conduit, from which the spiritual force of the mountain yogis spreads its influence into the plains, eventually reaching all the way down to Kanya Kumari at the tip of South India. The Ganga brings blessings not only to the areas along her banks but to the entire subcontinent. Feeling this spiritual current from the Himalayan heights added another dimension to my appreciation of the Vedic teachings.

During my first visit to Rishikesh we stayed at a place called Vedbhavan or the house of the Vedas. It was one of the oldest centers for Vedic rituals in the area, but had closed down its Vedic program in 1966 when the rich industrialists of the country ceased to lend their support for it. By chance I found myself at an old pillar of Vedic ritual.

Suvir Sharma, who now owned the place, was the last of that Vedic line raised to do Vedic chants and rituals. We listened as he chanted different Vedic styles from the *Rigveda* to the *Sāmaveda*. But unfortunately this tradition, like so many in India, appears nearing extinction. The demands of this commercial age have no real place for communing with the cosmic powers or for a life of ritual and chanting.

Uttar Kashi higher up from Rishikesh is the place where Shiva and Shakti unite. It has a special bliss and energy. There one can feel the power of the yogis and the presence of a culture of consciousness beyond the mundane world. In the Himalayas further up from there still reside many great and enigmatic yogis who will have nothing to do with the world. They preserve the spiritual heart of Hinduism, which so far remains in tact though perhaps in retreat. One can still meet with them and gain their grace if one makes the effort.

## Shankaracharyas

In the early nineties I came into contact with *Tattvaloka*, the journal of Sringeri Shankaracharya Math, through its editor T.R. Ramachandran, who took me on a special visit to Sringeri.

Sringeri is a hill station in Karnataka. It took several hours by car from the airport at Mangalore where we flew in. I was surprised to find the main center that the great Shankaracharya founded located in such a remote region. Clearly Shankara was more concerned with *tapas* than with gaining public acclaim. He was not creating a new religion that needed to convert the masses but a way of meditation in which we must work on ourselves. This is the Vedantic spirit, which one can still feel strongly at Sringeri. Self-development is the key to the Vedic spiritual path, not proselytizing.

I also came into contact with another Shankaracharya Math in Kanchipuram, a couple hours southwest of Chennai. Kanchipuram was one of the seven sacred cities of classical India and has many great temples.

Chandrashekhar Saraswati, the Shankaracharya at that time, was nearly a hundred years old and the grand old teacher of Hinduism. Fortunately I received his darshan twice before his death. He blessed the *rudrāksha-mālā* that is the main one that I use today. His work provides an excellent introduction to Hinduism, particularly in a Vedantic context.

A few years later through the intercession of the next Shankaracharya in the line, Jayendra Saraswati, I was able to visit the Kanchi Kamakshi temple and have a darshan of the Devi there, for which Westerners were usually not allowed. Such teachers continue to uphold Hindu Dharma and maintain millennial traditions for the benefit of future generations.

### Alandi – Swami Ram Das

Alandi near Pune in Maharashtra had a similar high spiritual vibration like the temple cities of South India and the Tīrthas of the North. There Jñānadeva who wrote the famous Jñānesvar commentary on the *Bhagavadgītā* was enshrined. He voluntarily went underground at the age of twenty one and never reappeared. The temple marks the tree beneath which he is said to be buried and will some day return from. Meditating there was a powerful experience and connected one with the great saints of Maharashtra, who did much to maintain Hinduism through the difficult period of Islamic rule.

Later I came into contact with the Samartha Ram Das order, from the great teacher who had been the guru of the Shivaji, the Maratha king who aroused the Hindus to revolt against the oppressive Mogul rule of the country. The Maratha power reclaimed most of India before the British conquered the country.

In time I had many such pilgrimages and experiences throughout India. These are just a few typical examples.

# 5

# Discovery of Social and Political Hinduism

## Encounter with Dr. B.L. Vashta

On my first trip to India I met an individual who would have a decisive influence on my life and thought. He would serve as my mentor for introducing me into Hindu thinking and to Hindu issues in India today. Dr. B.L. Vashta was an Ayurvedic doctor working on product development for an Ayurvedic company in Bombay. It was in that context in which I met him. He was then about seventy years of age or about the age of my father.

After chatting informally, we immediately felt a certain kinship. He inquired about my activities and interests and was curious about my work with the Vedas and ancient India. I would gradually develop a broad association with Vashta that would connect me to a whole network of Hindu organizations. We had long conversations over a wide variety of topics, mainly relative to India, Hinduism and the Vedas. We gradually developed a strategy to promote Vedic causes in both India and the West.

Vashta helped with my Ayurvedic work and introduced me to various Ayurvedic teachers and schools, particularly in nearby Pune. We attended several Ayurvedic conferences in places as far away as Bangalore and Madras. But Vashta was no mere Ayurvedic doctor. He was also an intellectual and a journalist and had been the editor of the famous *Kesri* newspaper of Pune for ten years. He wrote on religious and social issues as well and had authored many books and articles. He was one of the main Hindu writers in Maharashtra. Behind his humble demeanor he had a profound insight and an ability to help people connect to their deeper purpose in life.

Vashta first introduced me to local Hindu groups in Mumbai. These included regional branches of RSS (Rashtriya Swayamsevak Sangha), VHP (Vishwa Hindu Parishad), BJP (Bharatiya Janata Party) and their different affiliates, which up to that point I knew nothing about. I gradually learned about the Sangha Parivar or RSS family and its many affiliated organizations. Most of my work was with VHP, as it dealt more with religious issues, as the largest Hindu religious organization in the world.

I got to know many people in these organizations personally, including their leaders. I found them to be dedicated supporters of Hindu Dharma and protectors of Hindu society, as well as nationalistic Indians. Most were gentle and mild people like Vashta and were quite open-minded about religion and spirituality. Some like him had deep spiritual concerns and did intense *sādhanā*.

Vashta himself had been an RSS worker since the age of 18 or for nearly fifty years at the time. He introduced me to the work of various Hindu social and political writers like Tilak, Savarkar, and Guruji Golwalkar of RSS.

Lokamanya Tilak was the head of the Indian independence movement before Mahatma Gandhi. Tilak had a special interest in the Vedas and in the ancient history of India and wrote two important books on the subjects, the *Orion,* and the *Arctic Home in the Vedas.* I found Tilak's work on astronomical references in the Vedas via his *Orion* to be very crucial information for accurately dating the Vedas. However, I found his Arctic home theory to be farfetched, a product of the incomplete scientific information of his era.

I discovered that Tilak was closely connected with Aurobindo, who was his follower, and wanted Aurobindo to take over the independence movement after him. But Aurobindo had already retired from the world to do his yoga practice and decided against it. Both Tilak and Aurobindo found Mahatma Gandhi's insistence on non-violence to be excessive and wanted a more active campaign to oust the British.

Veer Savarkar was another Indian leader senior to Gandhi who was a firebrand revolutionary like those of Europe with whom he associated. He had a strong vision of Indian nationalism and was also not adverse to using force to remove the British. He was a deep thinker and a yogi in his later years. Unfortunately his work was denigrated and distorted by leftist opponents. There was a concerted effort to malign him as a Nazi because of his anti-leftist views, even though he was an opponent of Hitler and wanted India to join the war on the British side! Through Savarkar I gained a different idea of India's independence movement, which clearly was much more than the Gandhian images which is all that people in the West really know.

Guruji Golwalkar was the second head of the RSS after Hedgewar, who founded the organization in 1925. He was a mild mannered schoolteacher with a philosophical bent of mind. His main work is *Bunch of Thoughts*, which is a collection put together from his many talks and articles. In it I found a clear analysis of the social problems of Hinduism and of modern India with both practical and spiritual solutions to the problems. Golwalkar gave a clear critique of culture showing the dangers of materialism, Communism and missionary religions and suggested a dharmic alternative based upon Hindu and yogic teachings. The book was like an application of the thought of Vivekananda and Aurobindo to the social sphere. I was also surprised to know that such a deep and flexible approach was branded as fundamentalist by leftists in India.

Vashta also acquainted me with the work of Swami Dayananda Saraswati of the Arya Samaj, which added another dimension to my perspective on the Vedas. Swami Dayananda was the first modern teacher to go back to the Vedas and to unfold a purely spiritual interpretation of the older Vedic mantras. I realized that there was an entire Hindu social movement based upon return to the Vedas, a motto that I could follow as well.

Vashta admired Sri Aurobindo and looked to Ramana Maharshi as one of his gurus. He had a special connection with the Kanchi Shankaracharya Math and Swami Chandrashekhar Saraswati. But he had a broad approach not limited to a particular teacher or based on any personality cult. While Vashta knew the spiritual aspects of Hinduism, he was also aware of its social and political problems. He had his own spiritual insight and ability to judge and understand people that could be quite astounding.

Vashta himself was an intelligent, friendly and communicative person with a notable humility. In my years of association with him, I never saw him praise himself, promote himself or seek any personal advantage. On the contrary, he tried to protect me from Indians who might be seeking advantage from my work or from a connection with America. Nor did he ever seek to influence my opinions about Sangha groups, appealing to my emotions or trying to indoctrinate me. He simply introduced me to people or gave me information and encouraged me to make my own judgments. He was soft spoken and not inclined to exaggerate about anything. He was quite willing to admit the flaws or limitations in the organizations with which he worked.

Many young people would visit Vashta, who lived in a small flat in Santa Cruz, not far from the Mumbai airport. He would inspire and guide them in their lives and careers, with a notable practicality. He took a down to earth approach to the spiritual life, not trying to force anything but helping each person understand and follow his or her deeper nature. I felt that he gave me confidence in myself and in my deeper quest. He also provided a sense of community and common cause with many groups and took me out of the hermit-like isolation that had marked my previous years of private Vedic studies.

Once Vashta visited me in America. He enjoyed the space and beauty of the country, with its wide vistas, but sensed the loneliness and spiritual poverty of the culture. He also visited Germany as his daughter had married a German architect. He learned the German language and liked the culture, particularly thinkers like Goethe.

I visited Dr. Vashta many times over a ten year period and got to know both him and his family, who accepted me as one of their own. Together we watched my Vedic work in India develop from a mere idea to a significant influence, with many books and programs coming out. This was rewarding for both of us, as in the beginning we had no idea what the future would bring. We had the fortunate opportunity to see our work crowned with success in a period of only a few years.

The last time I saw Dr. Vashta was in the beginning of 1997. He was shifting from Mumbai to Pune, where he had built a retirement home. Under that pretext I stayed with him longer than usual and he passed on various books and papers to me. He was discarding what was inessential or complete and retiring to a more spiritual life.

After that a few months elapsed and I didn't receive any letters from him, which was unusual. Then I was awoke one night late after midnight. The thought came to me that Dr. Vashta might have passed away. He had a heart attack some years ago and his heart condition kept him from being very active. Sometimes I received phone calls from India late at night and wondered if I might soon receive one announcing his demise. That very moment the phone rang. A call came from friends in India giving the sad news that Vashta recently had died of a heart attack. It was in late July.

To deal with the emotion I took a drive up in to the

mountains, which are about half an hour by car from here. Next to the side of the road I suddenly saw a magnificent elk with large horns, something I have never seen in the mountains in many years. I felt that it indicated Vashta's soul, character and destiny.

## Anti-Hindu Media

When I was in India I read the English language newspapers, which were commonly available, particularly at the hotels where I sometimes stayed, and noted many of the magazines as well. I discovered that the press often spoke of the danger of "Hindu fundamentalism" referring mainly to RSS groups. The idea they projected was that such Hindu groups would oppress religious minorities, put an end to democracy and secularism in the country, and were dangerous, violent and bigoted.

According to *The Times of India* in Bombay, for example, RSS and its Sangha family were militant, fascist, and chauvinistic. I was both disturbed and perplexed by these remarks. Either my interaction with these Hindu groups was misleading or these negative opinions were totally wrong. Was I, a person of liberal and leftist views going back to my youth – a pacifist, vegetarian, and ecologist – becoming a stooge for right wing Hindus plotting pogroms against minorities in India, who if they came to power would create an oppressive and dictatorial state?

At the same time I noticed that the Indian newspapers would praise Islam and defend the cause of the Palestinians. One paper had an editorial on how an Islamic Republic was good for members of all religions, would protect minorities and was really the ideal system of government deriving from God. Of course, I was well aware of how intolerant such Islamic states as Saudi Arabia, Iran or Pakistan really were. That Hindus could praise the idea of an Islamic state and condemn Hindu political groups that were nowhere near as intolerant was amazing to me. There is no idea of a Hindu state, a Hindu law code, or a Hindu theocracy, nor any history of such comparable to the medieval ideal of a Christian state or the current idea, which is still medieval in nature, of an Islamic state.

The same newspapers praised Marx and Communism. They kowtowed to China and to the Soviet Union as the most progressive countries in the world. As Communism declined in Eastern Europe in the late eighties, they lamented the fact, and nostalgically hoped for a restoration of Communist rule. When there was an attempted coup in Russia in 1991 to overthrow Gorbachov and restore Communism, the then Congress led government of P.V. Narasimha Rao quickly recognized the coup leaders as the new Russian government, only to quickly withdraw its remarks in embarrassment when the coup failed. It seemed that Indian intellectuals transferred their loyalty from London to Moscow or Beijing but never placed it in Delhi or anywhere else in India or its traditions!

I had already learned how much the Vedas and the history of India had been distorted by Western scholars. Their missionary and colonial biases, as well as their lack of insight into spiritual traditions and symbols made their work more a mockery of the teachings than any real understanding. Sri Aurobindo once remarked that their work was comparable to kids playing with marbles outside the gates of a temple, totally unaware of the inner sanctuary. That this modern mindset might denigrate Hindu social or political movements was something to be expected. So when I saw the English language media of India criticizing Hindu social groups I took it all with a grain of salt, like their uncritical embracing of the Aryan invasion theory. Perhaps if I did not have such a background in the Vedas or a personal contact with Hindu groups, I might have taken the propaganda against them seriously, which many people, even those who have a regard for Indian traditions, seem to uncritically do.

I gradually began to see another side of the Indian mind, a modern intellectual side influence by the West, anti-spiritual, materialistic and hostile to its own traditions. Westerners, with their image of India as the land of yoga and meditation, are seldom aware of this Westernized Indian mind or how inimical it is to the very traditions that they are interested in. These same Indian leftists regard all Westerners interested in spiritual India as deluded, as representing a backward trend in Western culture!

With Vashta's help I visited with some leftist journalists and got to know their thinking first hand. He didn't provide any background on their views but allowed me to discover directly what motivated them. I gradually discovered the leftist influences behind such anti-Hindu propaganda as targeted the RSS. Indian leftists were naively idealistic about Communism, which they uncritically lauded with an almost Hindu devotion, turning Marx, Lenin, Stalin and Mao into gods and their writings into scriptures. Little did they know if there had been a real Communist revolution in India as there was in Russia, such intellectuals would have been among the first to be eliminated or at least condemned to manual labor as during the Cultural Revolution in China.

I remember visiting with a famous Indian Marxist poet in Mumbai. I questioned him why Indians, with such a great spiritual heritage and thinkers with cosmic vision from the Vedic Rishis onward, could be so enamoured of a simple materialist like Marx, who was a second hand thinker imitating Hegelian thought, which itself was spiritually naive? He replied, on the contrary, that he thought Hindu philosophy was a kind of double speak and mumbo jumbo which destroyed rational thinking and bound people to superstition and backwardness like the caste system.

Yet his comments revealed a glaring contradiction in his personal life. He lamented that for all his leftist writings and scholarship, his own wife was still a devotee of Krishna and the *Bhagavadgītā* was her favorite book. To him the *Gītā* was all Maya with its everything is Brahman. But for all his sharp intellect he couldn't even change his own wife's thoughts. He compared Hindu groups like RSS to Islamic Iran and the Ayatollah. That the Ayatollah more resembled a Josef Stalin didn't seem to dawn on him.

Over time I looked into these Hindu organizations to find these so-called intolerant and militant elements. I have never found them even until today. The most I found was an occasional perhaps overly sharp rhetoric, particularly against Islam, but even that was generally not inaccurate but at most unkind. The media exaggerated or even invented the charge of militance against Hindu groups, which were largely pacifistic and service oriented. The only exception was not the RSS but Shiva Sena who could be quite militant. But even they were largely defending their own culture and traditions.

I felt if this is all the India media has to worry about in terms of Hindu bigots, they have gotten off easily. All the Sangha groups and their leaders, their prejudices and fanatics included, are much more tolerant in religious views than your ordinary Christian and Muslim with their one prophet-savior, one holy book, salvation for the faithful and damnation for those of other beliefs. The average missionary is much more hardhearted and closed minded about other religions than the most dedicated RSS workers.

The VHP, particularly in America, created forums for religious understanding, regularly bringing Christian, Islamic and Jewish speakers to their conferences, emphasizing the commonality of all mystical traditions, something that Christian or Islamic groups would never do anywhere. That such broadminded people were branded narrow fundamentalists demonstrates the extent of anti-Hindu prejudice in the world. A Hindu accepting many paths and religions is branded an extremist if he wants to preserve his traditions and questions attempts to convert him. But a Christian or a Muslim actively trying to convert Hindus, negatively stereotyping the religion as pagan or polytheist, is considered progressive. It seemed to me at the time in India that just to call oneself a Hindu was enough to get branded a Hindu fundamentalist!

I propose a simple litmus test on fundamentalism. Ask a person whether they think that there are many paths to God and that no single religion, teacher or book has the last word on the matter. Ask them if there should be a free diversity of spiritual teachings in the world and that no single faith should try to convert the world to its belief. If the person insists upon one religion alone as true, then he is a fundamentalist. If he accepts many paths, then he is not. By this test few Hindus, even VHP or RSS members, would be fundamentalists, while few Christians and Muslims, particularly their main leaders, would not be.

## RSS and the Propaganda Against It

RSS is a service organization, promoting education, charity and Hindu cultural development. Its daily *Shākhā* meetings have a certain discipline, with a saluting of the flag and a promotion of nationalism, but no real militance. Its brand of Indian nationalism, recognizing cultural and religious pluralism, is more tolerant than most American nationalism. The organization is free of caste and members are not judged by their material status. While members honor their RSS leaders there is no personality cult of a charismatic leader dominant but rather a general sense of organizational strength, an almost anonymity about one's personal efforts and achievements.

Over time I visited various RSS related or founded organizations from intellectual groups to schools and hospitals to yoga institutions. All had dedicated workers and a very broad and diverse range of activities. All showed quite a diversity of opinions among their members. There was nothing like a party line in any of them.

Each group though part of the RSS family had a certain independence and was free to pursue its own goals without interference from the rest of the organization. There was little regimentation in thinking, action or even appearance, no central authority, church or dogma of any type. RSS groups included everyone and everything as long as there was a purpose to uplift the nation or to help people. It honored the great sages and rishis of India from Vedic times to the modern age, including Buddhist, Jain, Sikh and even some liberal Muslims.

Sangha members had a wide range of religious views from almost atheists to swamis. I met Sangha members who were strongly anti-Gandhi to those who greatly honored him. I met those who were staunch capitalists and others that were almost socialists. The Sangha discipline allowed for free-thinking, including internal criticism.

Such experiences made me think that Indian journalists were living in a totally unreal world. If there were real Hindu militants like Islamic militants such as Hamas, these journalists would not be able to make their criticisms at all. They would really be targeted and threatened! I realized that Indian journalists would denigrate Hindu activists in the media, knowing quite well that they would not be attacked in return. To date there has been no shutting down of newspapers by any RSS related group.

One of their main distortions that the media continually promoted in the media was that RSS killed Mahatma Gandhi. This was because Godse, Gandhi's murderer, had been a member of RSS and of the Hindu Mahasabha that was related to it. That the RSS was officially cleared of all such charges in court, which the great Indian leader Sardar Patel acknow-ledged, was ignored. That Godse had also been a Congress member was never mentioned. That he had left RSS because he felt that the group was too mild in its views was similarly not noted. I saw how such deceptions were perpetrated on uninformed readers and realized that such statements were often deliberate lies. The level of political corruption, political propaganda and media manipulation in India on such issues far exceeds that in America.

A similar piece of propaganda was that RSS members were

Nazi sympathizers. The brother of the revolutionary Savarkar and an associate of Golwalkar of RSS made some statements in the late thirties before World War II praising Germany, which are still promoted today as representing RSS views. That such views were common at the time, when even the Soviet Union signed a non-aggression pact with Hitler is ignored. That Savarkar encouraged India to join the British in the war against Germany and beseeched Hindus to join the British army, while Mahatma Gandhi started his Quit India movement and opposed the war effort, is also forgotten. Unfortunately, most people, particularly in the West, know so little about India that they can be easily deceived by such emotional appeals. After all, who likes Nazis? Christian, Islamic and Marxist groups pick these ideas up for their propaganda value.

That Hindus use the swastika, which is a traditional emblem of good fortune, and call themselves Aryans, something that Buddhists and Jains also do, calls up the European experience of the Nazis who distorted these terms. Unfortunately, the Nazi stereotype has become so ingrained in the mind of Western people that they are suspicious of any Hindu politics, even though the Nazis were predominantly Christians and had no Hindus among them! They see the Hindu swastika and associate it with Nazism! Indian leftists use this Nazi bogey to denigrate any Hindu resurgence that would threaten them. It is odd that pacifistic and tolerant Hindus are branded as militant Nazis because the Nazis distorted a few of their terms! Meanwhile Indian Marxists still honor Stalin and Mao, who can only compare with Hitler in regard to the genocide that they perpetrated and they are regarded in India as liberal and secular people.

**Dealing with Caste**

One of the most difficult issues for modern Hinduism is the problem of caste. Hinduism has been stereotyped as a caste religion in which family of birth is more important than any individual merit. This anti-caste sentiment has been the main vehicle of anti-Hindu propaganda. Whether it is leftists, Christians or Muslims when you mention Hinduism, it is not Yoga and Vedanta with their universal spiritual vision that they emphasize but caste, as if there was nothing more to Hinduism.

Caste or *varṇa* originally refers to the four divisions of traditional Hindu society as the Brahmin or priestly class, the Kshatriya or noble class, the Vaishya or merchant class and the Shudras or servant class. Originally it was a threefold division of the priests, nobility and common people. The word Vaishya for the merchant class derives from Vish, which means people in general. The Vaishyas were also divided into the merchants proper and the farmers. Apart from these four castes was a fifth or mixed caste. Similar social orders dominated the ancient and medieval worlds, like the European division of the priests, nobility, merchants and common people or peasants. Though in the modern world caste appears backwards it was probably inevitable given the social and material circumstances of these previous eras.

These castes in India were not rigid and allowed for an upward movement. Women could marry up in caste and their children's caste would become that of their father. Castes could fall in status, as when a Brahmin family had to take on non-Brahmanical occupations like becoming merchants. In Vedic times individuals who demonstrated the ability could rise in caste as well. Moreover, to become a monk in Hinduism one always has had to renounce all caste identity.

The Hindu caste or *varṇa* system, moreover, is very different than the European class system. The Brahmins or priestly class were wedded to a life of austerity and learning and not allowed to accumulate wealth or power. The exceptions were the royal Brahmins who were in the service of the kings. They sometimes acted as political and legal advisors. They were often given large land grants to found schools and temples. Unfortunately, some of them fell from the required austerity of their class and began to function more like landowners. A few Brahmins also took on Kshatriya roles and became kings. This was allowed as an exception if the Kshatriya class failed at its duties.

However, the average village Brahmin or temple priest has remained to the present day, a poor scholar, teacher or ritualist, working in the service of the community for a menial subsistence. The temple priests of South India today are among the poorest of the poor.

The Marxist propaganda of the Brahmins as the wicked landowners oppressing the poor untouchables, is an exaggeration that is seldom true. Most of the landowners in India are not Brahmins, which was never their traditional occupation. In classical India few groups aspired to become Brahmins any more than the average medieval European peasant wanted to become a priest. The powerful Kshatriya or the wealthy Vaishya was the social ideal.

I remember when a Western friend first came to India, he saw porters carrying luggage for wealthier Indians and remarked how the Brahmins were still using the poorer people as servants. Though he was not a leftist, he was so influenced by the anti-Brahmin propaganda that he assumed that the rich people were Brahmins and their wealth was based on caste, which was not the case at all. When I informed him of his error he was surprised.

Untouchability is also misunderstood. It was originally a matter of social purity, reflecting the principle of non-violence. Brahmins could not eat out of utensils in which meat or other impure food articles had been cooked. This led to a ban on eating with non-Brahmins, particularly those who had impure forms of livelihood like butchers. This led eventually to a ban on association with such people.

Untouchability arose from an excessive pursuit of purity, like the purity of a monk who could not associate with those who worked in bars or taverns. Unfortunately this untouchability became extreme and has become a bane on Hindu society. But it is hardly the same situation as the rich European aristocracy who would not mingle with peasants. Caste as this traditional *varṇa* system hardly exists in India today anyway. Most Brahmins today do not follow Brahmanical occupations like temple priests, though most do promote good education in their families. The same is true of the other castes. Most Kshatriyas are not in military, police or government service. A number of Shudra groups are quite wealthy, particularly in South India. But the poor and untouchables still remain, kept up not only by social prejudices but also by a high birth rate. While the educated in India as throughout the world have fewer children, the uneducated still have many. So the caste problem is also a problem of poor education and overpopulation. The best way to address it is not by promoting caste divisions but by directly tackling these overriding problems.

Modern India is divided not so much by caste as by family or tribe (*jāti*). Different families, communities and regional groups promote their own particular interests over that of the nation. This phenomenon starts with the Nehru family itself, which has tried to dominate the country like a monarchy with an hereditary right to rule, in the meantime amassing wealth and power for itself. Such family divisions are responsible for the many regional political parties that exist in India today as well as the demands for special rights and reservations for various communities. This divisive thinking is the real problem, not the Vedic *varṇas*. It destroys any feeling of national unity and causes people to seek to take advantage of the government for their personal ends.

**Royal Asiatic Society**

I particularly remember speaking before the Royal Asiatic Society in Bombay, which was organized by friends at *Vivek* Weekly, a Hindu journal. I spoke on India and its Vedic heritage and the need for its revival in the modern world. The discussion helped me understand how much the Marxists dominated the society. One of the women on the dais who was eminent in the society brought up the issue of the law of karma during the question and answer period. She asked, "Wasn't the law of karma invented by the Brahmins for purposes of caste exploitation?"

I was surprised by her statement. It amazed me to think that any educated person in India could ask such a question. I learned that most of the intellectuals of India were so Westernized and alienated from their own traditions that they only looked at them with suspicion and disdain, looking for such worldly motives in Hindu spirituality.

The other leader of the Society himself tried to portray me as a holdover from the sixties in America. He appeared disturbed by my statements praising the Vedas or the favorable crowd reaction to my speech. He talked of Indian gurus coming to the West as merely looking for money and people like myself as perhaps well-meaning but intellectually naive.

I had remarked that such thinkers as Marx were rather minor figures compared to such Indians as Sri Aurobindo or Vivekananda who could place all these Western intellectuals in one corner of their minds. This is certainly true. Why an Indian would not feel proud of such a truth but feel sympathy towards Marx and his followers is the real mystery, but it is quite common in the country. Later someone told me that Indians have a soft spot for Karl Marx. Be careful criticizing him in public talks I was told. I gave many such talks and had similar experiences.

## Reimportation

I usually received a warm welcome, a favorable response and good audiences during my many India talks. At first I groped for the words and ideas to communicate to a Hindu audience. I wondered if they could understand my English or follow my American accent. But I discovered that most of them understood what I said. Soon I had no trouble talking before Indian audiences. I eventually found it easier than talking to American audiences, whose interest in Vedic matters was very limited.

One person in the audience during a talk in Bombay made the important statement that "We in India appreciate something only when its been reimported." It is odd that what a Westerner says about Hinduism is taken more seriously in India than what a better qualified traditional Hindu would say. Something said by a Westerner is taken as unbiased, while a traditional Hindu is not credited with any objectivity and his opinion is given no worth. Actually the opposite case is usually true. The Westerner is usually following a religious, commercial or political bias that he may not even be aware of. Many Hindus are quite objective even about their own tradition, while at the same time understanding the limitations of Western culture. This is particularly true of Swamis of the Advaita Vedanta order from the South India from whom I have heard profound analyses of the world situation today.

Still the example of someone from the West promoting Vedic knowledge may have a salutary effect on modern Hindus, who are used to looking to the West for cultural innovations. More Westerners should do this if they want to see Eastern traditions survive the onslaught of Western culture. Several Westerners living in India are already quite active in such work, particularly disciples of Sri Aurobindo from France. Some like Francois Gautier and Michel Danino have written books and articles that eloquently deal with the need for a resurgent Hinduism.

While Western yoga students sometimes find my comments about the political situation in India to be too pro-Hindu, this is seldom the case with Westerners actually living in India, particularly those working in the religious field. They have to deal first hand with the leftist propaganda and missionary aggression, and have understood the media distortions. They see with their own eyes the modern cultural war in which Hindu society is under siege by vested interests of less tolerant and more materialistic forces.

The example of Western Swamis can be very helpful, showing to Hindus how Western people can dedicate their lives to Hindu spirituality. One Western Swami in India that has strongly encouraged my defense of Hinduism is Swami Satyananda. Originally from Spain he became a Swami under Muktananda. Later he lived at the Ramanashram for many years, performing the full range of *tapas*. He also did pilgrimages throughout India and to Mount Kailas in Tibet. Now he looks like a great Rishi and shows how even Westerners can advance on the yogic path if they faithfully follow its disciplines.

Swami Satyananda has continued to encourage my work upholding Hindu Dharma. Whenever I feel isolated or extreme in my views I remember such examples. I have also at times considered becoming a Swami myself but at least for now have decided against it in order to have more freedom of action and expression in political and intellectual fields, which is usually outside the field of concern for renunciates.

**Not so Good Hindus**

My admiration for Hindu Dharma was never a mindless and uncritical admiration of all Hindus or of all Indian society. Even among otherwise good or insightful Hindus I sometimes found negative character and personality traits. It seems that Hindus were often their own worst enemies. Westerners provided an easy way to make money for some of them and they exploited this as best they could, including using a spiritual appearance in order to do so.

Some Hindus who uncritically fancied themselves spiritual or enlightened dispensed with human decency along the way. They indulged in negative gossip and sought to defame their competition, even their students who might stand on their own. It is easy to turn oneself into a guru and then place one's behavior beyond scrutiny, focusing on the faults of others rather than on improving oneself. But the true Hindu way is one of self-introspection in which we examine our own faults before casting a critical eye on others. And it is not the personality of the other that we should find fault with but wrong doctrines that distort the soul, which is good, divine and wonderful in all creatures.

My appreciation of Hinduism was never blind or the result of any personality worship. Hinduism as an open tradition has room for everything, even a fair amount of wishful thinking. Its highest truth is the Self, the real individual, which should never be made subordinate to any external authority, idea, emotion or imagination.

## Becoming Vamadeva Shastri

In 1991 Dr. Vashta raised the idea that I formally become a Hindu. I thought, Why not? I have been following this tradition for twenty years and working with it had become my main spiritual path and career dedication. I thought about the many Hindus that have become Christians following the allure of the affluent West. The example of a Christian becoming a Hindu would be good for many Hindus and would encourage confidence in their own traditions.

Why shouldn't I express my appreciation and make a more formal connection with Hindu Dharma? Personally, I am not much for formality and generally avoid ceremony or any kind of outer displays. But it didn't take much forethought to go ahead with this important project. It was also a way to create a new identity for myself that reflected the changes that I had gone through internally.

Dr. Vashta told me that I was already a Hindu inwardly and so an outward ceremony wasn't necessary, but that the gesture would be appreciated by the community. I understood. The ceremony was called Shuddhi, which means purification. It was short and simple, a ritual puja, a *kumbha abhishekam*. It was held at a local Mumbai ashram, Masur Ashram that had once been connected to the Arya Samaj but in time became more traditionally Hindu. No preaching. No condemnation. No threats or promises. No swearing to go to a particular church or follow a prescribed path of action. Just a promise to follow dharma.

While Vashta organized the event, Avadhuta Shastri, the head of Masur Ashram, performed the puja. His brother Brahmachari Vishwanath was one of the founders of the VHP. I took the name Vamadeva from the Vedic Rishi Vamadeva Gautama. Shastri came from Avadhuta Shastri.

I first noted the name Vamadeva while studying the Upanishads. The *Brihadāraṇyaka Upanishad* quotes Rishi Vamadeva for the great saying (*mahāvākya*) *Aham Brahmo'smi* (I am Brahman or I am God). This it relates to Vamadeva's saying in the *Rigveda*, "I was Manu and I became the Sun" (IV.26.1).

The *Aitareya Upanishad* mentions Vamadeva, who was said to have learned the Vedas while still within his mother's womb. It quotes another statement of Vamadeva from the *Rigveda* (IV.27.1), "When I was in my mother's womb I learned the birth of all the Gods."

Among the first hymns of the *Rigveda* whose inner meaning became clear to me were those of Brihadukta, the son of Vamadeva (RV X.54-56). Others were hymns of Vamadeva himself, which comprise most of the fourth book of the *Rigveda,* particularly his hymns to Agni and Indra, such as Sri Aurobindo also specially admired.

Vamadeva was an unusual and mysterious Rishi, ascribed with an almost miraculous birth. Vamadeva and his *gotra* (family), the Gotamas, were associated with the land of Videha in Bihar and Nepal from which Sita came and which was the home of the great royal-sages, the Janakas, on which many Upanishads like the *Brihadāraṇyaka*, and Advaitic works, like the *Ashtāvakra Gītā,* were based. The first· mentioning of Sita as an earth Goddess occurs in the hymns of Vamadeva in the *Rigveda* (IV.57). Many teachings are ascribed to dialogues between Vasishtha, *purohita* of Kosala, and Vamadeva, *purohita* of nearby Videha, including teachings on Astrology and on Ayurveda.

Vamadeva was a name of Indra, the supreme Vedic God, particularly as a falcon (*śyena*). It was also a name of Savitar, the Sun God, who dispensed his grace or beauty (*vāma*). Vamadeva later became a name of Lord Shiva in his northern face. So it was an important and powerful name and one that few people carried.

By this ceremony I was accepted into Hindu society as a Brahmin by my occupation. I realized that I was a kind of Kshatriya as well, a warrior at least on the intellectual plane, addressing not only religious but also social and political issues.

## Vedantic, Vedic, Hindu

Becoming a Hindu was the third stage in my inner transformations after becoming a Vedantin and then a Vedic person. It was another difficult and slow change with no real example to follow. While there were many more Hindus than Vedic or Vedantic votaries, few Westerners had taken this approach. I found myself breaking new ground with no one really to show the way. But perhaps because of the uniqueness of what I was trying to do, there was much interest in it in India and much support came from different areas.

I gradually came to understand the same sense of truth and universality that I saw in Veda and Vedanta extending to all aspects of Hindu culture. The term Hindu ceased to be a narrow or derogatory designation and became a term of respect and universality, the modern name of Sanātana Dharma, the eternal tradition of truth. I saw a resurrection of Hindu Dharma as central to world spirituality for the new global age.

# 6

# Journalistic Work

I have always written about whatever subjects I studied from poetry and philosophy to medicine and astrology. Not surprisingly Dr. Vashta encouraged me to write a series of articles on issues facing Hinduism today. I had an inside position on these topics that few Westerners had access to. Answering his request I wrote a series of articles in 1989. Of these most notable was a short piece called "Arise Arjuna", which appeared in late 1989 in the twenty-fifth anniversary issue of *Hindu Vishva*, the journal of the Vishva Hindu Parishad.

The same trend developed back in America. In 1991 I wrote several pieces for *India Times,* a small Indo-American newspaper, starting with a short article on the Myth of the Aryan Invasion. My articles eventually appeared in a number of Indo-American newspapers including *News India Times* and *India Post*. Other Indo-American publications like *India West* gave favorable reviews of my books.

Shortly thereafter I began to submit articles to the *Organiser,* the main English language publication for the RSS in India, and became a regular contributor. In time I wrote for many other publications in India as well. This began my career as a Hindu journalist, which I never planned or got paid for.

## Voice of India: Ram Swarup and Sita Ram Goel

Ram Swarup is probably the most important and cogent writer on Hinduism in the last half of the twentieth century. He is the inspirational force behind Voice of India, a small publishing company that has produced many well-documented works on Hinduism and its relationship with other religions. Voice of India has published perhaps the best series of books in defense of Hindu Dharma ever produced. Even larger Hindu organizations like RSS or Arya Samaj have not been able to create works of such detail or insight.

Voice of India does not take an apologetic tone or aim at any superficial religious synthesis, unlike most presentations of Hinduism. It reflects a critical Hindu point of view on the world with a rare examination of anti-Hindu forces, their history, plans and motivations. It has a fearlessness, honesty and truthfulness that rarely exists in modern Hindu writers who prefer to please everyone or harmonize all points of view rather than take a tough stand for what is right.

The main limitation that I found in Sangha groups, which Sangha people like Dr. Vashta concurred with, was that they lacked sophistication in their intellectual presentation, particularly in a modern English idiom. They emphasized grass root action instead and did not always think it important. This made them an easy target of the highly Westernized and well-educated leftist media in India. It also limited their appeal to the intellectuals of the country who were looking for sharp thinking and new ideas. With Voice of India I found a committed Hindu intelligentsia that took up all the difficult issues and clearly articulated them.

While Voice of India had a controversial reputation, I found nothing irrational, much less extreme about their ideas or publications. They were simply doing for the Hindu religion what intellectuals in other religious traditions had done for theirs. Their criticisms of Islam were on par with the criticisms of the Catholic Church and of Christianity done by such Western thinkers as Voltaire or Thomas Jefferson. In fact they went far beyond such mere rational or historical criticisms of other religions and brought in a profound spiritual and yogic view as well. They were only controversial because, since such a Hindu point of view had not been previously articulated, its sudden occurrence was threatening to non-Hindu groups.

I had already seen several Voice of India books when I first came into contact with Ram Swarup through correspondence. I first visited him during a trip to Delhi in 1992. My meeting with Ram Swarup was another significant event, similar to my meeting with Dr. Vashta. His book *The Word As Revelation: Names of Gods* was most interesting to me because it reflected a similar research into the Vedas that I had engaged in. It set the stage for our encounter.

Ram Swarup was a gentle and humble man, with a notable sweetness of character. In some ways he was like a great sage. In other ways he was almost childlike. He had no consciousness of money, fame or power. He was like a sannyasin but apart from any monastic order and not trying to build up any ashram or mission. Yet he was also a sharp and focused intellectual who penetrated to the core of an issue and established the key insights about it. He was inspired by Aurobindo both for his social and his spiritual views, though he had his own mind and was never an imitator of anyone.

Originally Swarup was one of the main writers in India to oppose Communism. This was in the fifties and sixties when Communism was fashionable in the country and favored by the then Prime Minister Jawaharlal Nehru. Few dared to challenge this totalitarian ideology in India and none so incisively as Swarup.

Ram Swarup later produced a remarkable and honest analysis of Christianity and Islam from a spiritual and psychological point of view. This he gave in his classic book *Hindu View of Christianity and Islam,* which not only Hindus but members of all religions should read. The book has helped many people look clearer at these religions, their history and their motivation, which is often quite different from the meditative religions of the East.

Swarup discerned a lower psychic formation behind these credal religions that turned them into mass movements and caused them to seek world domination. He showed how these religions lack an interior dimension. They emphasize not in *sādhanā* or self-development but the need to impose their views on others. Such creeds do not have a clear understanding of karma or self-realization but hold that a mere change of belief can really transform people. The result is that they hypnotize their followers with a belief, who then lose the power to critically examine what they are doing or how they might be harming others. Just think of all the professional people in the world today who uncritically accept such religious dogmas as the Biblical view of creation as literally true!

Religion creates a strong psychic force, energizing the subtle bodies of its believers with powerful *saṁskāras* born of prayer, ritual and group action. This force, if compassionate in nature, can lead to a higher consciousness, but if it reflects any exclusivism or prejudice it can bring out some of the worst traits in human nature, including violence and genocide. Religion magnifies our *saṁskāras* for good or ill. Otherwise quite balanced and sensitive people can lose all sense of objectivity when religion comes into the matter. Religious self-righteousness is perhaps the most destructive force that the human race has ever invented and continues to prey upon helpless victims all over the world.

The nature of a particular religion's psychic force depends upon the *guṇas* or qualities that it is based on. *Sāttvika* teachings promote love, compassion, non-violence, tolerance and a respect for different beliefs. *Rājasika* religions reflect a mentality of aggression and pride seeking to conquer the world for the true faith. *Tāmasika* religions are mired in superstition, prejudice, hatred and fanaticism. If a religion has strong *rājasika* or *tāmasika* elements than these will eventually come out in the psyche of its believers and lead them to destructive behavior. It can result in mob action in which people lose their reason, feeling and compassion.

Spiritual development is not a major concern in the West,

where the main attention is given to the outer life. The result is that Western religions are encased in darkness (*tamas*), persisting more as a remnant of a former age than anything creative and alive. In fact we let survive in the form of religion prejudices and superstitions what we have otherwise banished long ago (like a naïve belief in miracles or fantasies of an eternal heaven and hell).

The missionary is usually a person motivated not by love of God or love of humanity, but by an intolerant belief that won't let him rest in peace until the entire world takes to his brand of religion. Mental states born of religious exclusivity are agitated and turn into disturbed states of mind. Dogmatic religious beliefs encourage behavior on a mass level that would be neurotic or psychotic on an individual level.

I have thought of the many Christian and Islamic missionaries who came to India throughout the centuries and have utterly missed the spiritual greatness of Hindu Yoga and Vedanta traditions, thinking that all Hindus were mere heathens or *kafirs* going to hell without their help. Such missionaries tried to convert the great Hindu yogis or saints they encountered, utterly missing their spiritual attainments.

The Muslims have been in India for over a thousand years and still lack the most elementary understanding of the Hindu yogic path. They reject karma and rebirth as superstitions, and look at the many wonderful Hindu Gods and Goddesses that connect us to the cosmic mind as little better than demons. Their mullahs encourage such attitudes in order to keep them separate from Hindus and unable to interact with them on religious issues.

The British, with all their intellectual acumen, were in India for over two hundred years and left with no real understanding of the spiritual depths of the country. Their concern was money and hegemony, not enlightenment and higher consciousness. Such people have their minds closed in a narrow belief. Like a blind person they miss the obvious even when it stares right in their face. Many modern Indian intellectuals are of the same ilk; conditioned by Marx, Max Müller and Macaulay they cannot appreciate an Aurobindo or a Ramana Maharshi.

Ram Swarup, however, never turned his critical statements into any blanket condemnations. He judged individuals in their own right. He dialogued with people of all religious persuasions and would give any person a fair hearing. There was no partiality in him but a respect for truth above all other concerns.

I followed Ram Swarup's insights in my own writings, noting not only a spiritual (*daivika*) but also an egoistic or *āsurika* factor in mysticism that I highlighted in my book *Awaken Bharata*. Religion can project cosmic forces not only of light and knowledge but also of darkness and ignorance. Religious states of mind can augment pride or confuse the ego with God. Spirituality is a domain that has great dangers as well as great opportunities for the soul. Unless we approach it with critical insight and self-introspection we may get caught in various illusions or prejudices that will cause more harm than good.

Ram Swarup was not alone in his work but had an able colleague and friend who complemented his work on many levels. Sita Ram Goel was actually the main writer in Voice of India. He was a more researched scholar than Ram Swarup and produced many more books. Sita Ram followed a strong rationalistic point of view that did not compromise the truth even for politeness sake. His intellectual rigor is quite unparalleled in Hindu circles where soft, syncretic and apologetic tones prevail. He took Ram Swarup's key insights and developed them into a profound and incisive historical and political analysis.

I admired Sita Ram's honesty, directness of expression and fearlessness. He complemented the mystical vision of Ram Swarup with a practical side. He would not compromise truth for anything. He wouldn't bow down before any personalities, however great, or indulge in hyperbole and fantasy like many Hindus. Nor would he seek to escape from existent problems into some idealistic future. He remained focused on actual issues and dealt with them with detail and depth.

At first I was shocked to read his work *Hindu Temples, What Happened to Them.* I didn't' realize how much religious aggression had been perpetrated against the spiritual land of India where all religion is honored. I had felt that Islam, though perhaps young and immature as a religion, was really benign. But the evidence was overwhelming as Sita Ram used Islamic sources that had no reason to hide anything. There was a concerted campaign to destroy Hindu temples in India that most Islamic rulers in the country diligently followed.

Nor is the battle over. The fundamentalist Islamic movement that has spawned the Taliban and Osama Bin Laden still targets Hindu India and regards it as a land of *kāfirs* (heathens). It wants to finish the work of conquering the country and eliminating its infidel ways. Unless Hindus are more wary, they can be again deceived and defeated, and their heritage will be lost for all time.

Voice of India also published the works of Koenraad Elst, a young Belgian writer whom I met on several occasions. Elst intrigued me because he was a Westerner yet had a grasp of India better than any Indian did. In this regard I saw a parallel phenomenon to myself. But Elst had much better command of political and social issues in India than I ever gained, unmatched by any Western writer and researched in great detail. Elst is a thorough scholar and supremely rational in all that he does. His work on the Ayodhya movement was definitive.

**Writing for Voice of India**

I soon realized that there was a dearth of writers from a Hindu point of view in readable modern English. I decided to publish several books with Voice of India, starting with a shortened version of my historical study of ancient India. I called it the *Myth of the Aryan Invasion* and it was first published in late 1994. I thought such a short work would have an easier access in India because it would be very inexpensive. I also became inspired to write longer works on Hinduism. I took a collection of my articles and put them together as *Arise Arjuna: Hinduism and the Modern World* (1995). This was my first social-political-journalistic book. Its theme came from the short article "Arise Arjuna". It included a number of articles that I had done on various topics.

I wrote a book specifically on Hinduism called *Hinduism, the Eternal Tradition* (1995), which followed the line of thinking of Ram Swarup and was done according to his suggestion. This included questions and answers on relevant topics, including a Hindu response to common criticisms leveled against it.

These books brought a greater sense of responsibility upon me because they influenced people on a more vital and emotional level than simple books on health or spirituality that I had already written. At the same time they were more engaging and helped catalyze more significant changes in my own psyche.

A few years later I added *Awaken Bharata* that continued the themes of *Arise Arjuna*. I took a tone not simply to inform but also to motivate and to inspire. Hindus not only lack the information but also lack the will to stand up and present their views, however salutary, in the modern world. They have been too beaten down by centuries of foreign rule and also confused by their own efforts to equate all religions regardless of their actual practices and beliefs.

I hoped to energize a *samkalpa-shakti* or will power among Hindus and a *sangha-shakti* or power of association to bring it about. Fortunately I was able to get Ram Swarup to write the forward to this book as he passed away within the year. He left a profound gap in Hindu thought that will only

with difficulty find another spokesperson of such a caliber.
My journalistic work became read by a number of important Hindu leaders, as well as Hindu thinkers from different backgrounds. This led to various contacts, conversations and new information from many sources. Eventually I met with various important journalists in India like Arun Shourie, S. Gurumurthy, Varsha Bhosle and others active in the field. Though a minority among journalists in India today they have produced important works on a wide variety of topics.

In the space of the last few years I have seen several new writers taking up similar themes, making this Hindu journalism into a real voice in the Indian media. But it has yet to overcome the more prevalent anti-Hindu tone even in India. I expect that this victory will be achieved within the next decade as we can now discern the light at the end of the tunnel.

### Ashok Chowgule – Hindu Vivek Kendra

I first met Ashok Chowgule in Mumbai in 1992, at the time that the Babri Masjid was demolished by Hindu groups. He came from a wealthy industrialist family but chose to devote his time to the VHP, eventually becoming the head of the organization for Maharashtra. Dr. Vashta first introduced me to him and encouraged our association.

Ashok quickly took to the cause of promoting Hindu points of view through the media and through the internet, through the website of Hindu Vivek Kendra. He put some of my books and articles on line as well. Such media work is crucial for bringing Hinduism into the computer age where its point of view needs to be expressed. Otherwise anti-Hindu distortions will uncritically be perpetuated.

### Hinduism Today

*Hinduism Today* is a magazine reporting Hindu Dharma in the broadest sense from social to spiritual issues. Surprisingly, it is run by Western swamis. *Hinduism Today* had a similar approach as the groups I was working with in India. I began a dialogue with them, mainly on historical issues but also on Ayurveda and Vedic astrology and eventually on conversion issues.

*Hinduism Today* was influenced by Ram Swarup and Sita Ram Goel. They called Ram Swarup, "Perhaps Hinduism's most cogent analyst." Subrahmanya Swami, the head and *sadguru* of the ashram, though born in the West, has come to embody the wisdom, virtues and ideals of Hinduism. He is an articulate writer and speaker on Hindu causes as his many books like *Dancing with Shiva, Merging with Shiva*, and *Loving Ganesha* so beautifully reveal. His Western swami disciples are of a similar caliber, combining discipline, insight and dedication. They are particularly alert on the issues of the missionaries and the mischief they are causing within Hindu society.

A few years later I visited their ashram in Hawaii, which is like a paradise, the astral plane on earth or *svarga-loka*. It is a Shangri-La like setting on Kauai, the oldest and most verdant of the lush Hawaiian Islands, with wonderful gardens, waterfalls and pools. There one experiences a futuristic Hinduism as well as one of the ancient past when the Earth was pure and the creation fresh. *Hinduism Today* is doing a remarkable work providing a forum for Hindus to communicate with each other and faithfully recording the renaissance of Hindu Dharma in the modern age. It is strange that Western Hindus are the first to overcome Hinduism's remarkable sectarianism and create such unity!

Unlike apologetic Hindus who shy away from the name Hindu, *Hinduism Today* proudly uses it, pointing out that its negative connotations are the product of missionary and colonial propaganda, much of it from the Christian schools in India that so many Hindus uncritically send their children to. A religion that is calmly sending its children to schools of a religion seeking to convert them surely needs some self-examination! *Hinduism Today* provides that.

I once had a powerful vision of Lord Hanuman in Kauai,

who clearly was angry. As the defender of nature and of the Earth (Sita), he is insisting that we change our ways and return to the kingdom of Rama (God) or much suffering is in store for us. Let us heed this warning of Hanuman! As the son of the Wind, the leader of the heavenly army, and the protector of the animals we can't afford to ignore his wishes.

**Prajna Bharati**

Once in Bombay we received a fax from a Hyderabad organization requesting my appearance as a speaker. This is how I came to know of Prajna Bharati. I first spoke in Hyderabad in 1996, giving programs on the Vedas at Prajna Bharati and on Ayurveda at Vijnana Bharati. The audience was quite large and the questions very profound. In 1997 I returned to help launch the first issue of *Prajñā*, a magazine for Prajna Bharati in Hyderabad and contributed regularly to that publication as well. Later in 1999 I did several programs for them, including a debate with the Archbishop of Hyderabad that appears later in this book.

Prajna Bharati is perhaps the best organized Hindu think tank and intellectual center in India. It brings together important thinkers on various topics, representing all sides, and creates a forum for dialogue, debate and discussion. Hopefully such centers will open throughout the country

**Bharatiya Janata Party**

Nor surprisingly, in the course of such interactions I came in contact with the BJP (Bharatiya Janata Party), another offshoot of RSS, and eventually met with several of its main leaders. I utterly failed to see how this political party was fundamentalist, much less dangerous. They were quite liberal in their views, but from a Hindu and dharmic perspective, rather than the standpoint of Western humanism. Though called right wing in the Indian media, most of their views like their support of vegetarianism, ecology, Yoga and Vedanta, and their resistance to Western consumerism would be regarded as left wing in America. I eventually wrote articles for *BJP Today* on social and political topics on issues from the elections to nuclear testing to missionary activity.

After their election victory in 1998, I met with such BJP leaders as L.K. Advani, the Home Minister, who had been introduced to my work by Girilal Jain. Advani remarked that the journalists and media people in India were still unwilling to accept that a BJP government had come to power and were doing all they could to malign and destabilize it. I noted how much both the Western and Indian media tried to denigrate this government, simply because it had honor and respect for the Hindu tradition.

## An Intellectual Kshatriya

When I was speaking in England on a tour for the VHP, needing to produce new talks on an almost daily basis, the idea of an intellectual Kshatriya came to me. The Kshatriyas were the traditional warrior class whose role was to defend Hindu society. In the modern age of the computer revolution and the information war I suggested that an intellectual Kshatriya was the need of the times. Hinduism has always been a religion of ideas and in this new age of information it can use the strength of its insights to overcome the inimical forces that have challenged it on a more outward level.

Sita Ram Goel got wind of the idea and asked me to develop it further. It eventually became the core of my book *Awaken Bharata*. This idea of an intellectual Kshatriya has become a theme for my writings on Hinduism. Such a new class is essential to protect Hindu society and its heritage and also to make it accessible for the rest of the world. Without these Kshatriyas Hinduism will remain under siege and even its great spiritual heritage will become eroded and lost. This idea of an intellectual Kshatriya has remained a theme of my work. The Vedas say that speech (*vāk*) is the weapon of the Brahmin. Such intellectual Kshatriyas are also Brahmana-Kshatriyas.

## Karma Yoga/Hindu Activism

My work with Hindus took me in the direction of Karma Yoga, which I had previously not well understood or appreciated. Karma Yoga is the first and most foundational of all the yogas. Life, after all, is action. Work is unavoidable. We should always be doing something, trying to progress spiritually or to help others. Otherwise we easily get caught in inertia and allow negative forces to advance. For any action, even meditation, to affect us at a deeper level it must follow a certain rhythm, regimen or repetition. It must be a karma and a *saṁskāra* (sacrament).

Karma Yoga is of two types: ritual worship of the cosmic powers (*Devatas*) and service to the world. True ritual worship is not merely mechanically performing pujas or mantras. It means right action following a right intention to bring a higher power of consciousness into life. All true spiritual practices rest upon a sense of service, not upon a seeking of one's personal gain as the main goal.

My spiritual path moved from Jñāna Yoga (Yoga of Knowledge) to Bhakti Yoga (Yoga of Devotion) and to Karma Yoga (Yoga of Action), not by rejecting the previous yogas but by integrating them into a more realistic approach. Only on a firm foundation of Karma Yoga or right action are real Bhakti and Jñāna possible as a way of transformation.

Karma Yoga as service to the world can be defined as "Hindu activism". This properly speaking is not serving any mere political, social or religious cause but upholding dharma in the world and promoting a spiritual culture. Without such Hindu activism Hindu Dharma remains lethargic and backward looking – contracted and unable to communicate its wisdom and energy in the modern context. This lack of Karma Yoga as an activist force has kept Hinduism in retreat and removed the insight of the Hindu mind from the world forum in which it is so desperately needed.

Karma Yoga or Hindu activism to some extent entered the Indian political arena during the independence movement. It now needs to emerge as a global force and power of conscience in dealing with the challenges of the post-industrial and post-colonial era in which a new planetary culture is required. May such a new Hindu activism arise, particularly among the youth!

## Becoming a Pandit

In 1996 I received the Brahmachari Vishwanathji Award in Mumbai, which recognized me as a Pandit and Dharmacharya. The award came from Masur Ashram, which had five years earlier given my Hindu name. This award formally took me from being a Hindu to being a Hindu teacher. It also came from Vashta's help to promote my work further. Such ceremonies empower a person, affording the support of a broader community so that one is not simply proceeding on one's own.

# 7

# Ancient India
# and Vedic Knowledge

## The Myth of the Aryan Invasion

The ancient world contained many spiritual wonders, magnificent temples, great pyramids, secret knowledge and enlightened sages. It was not the primitive era that our history books proclaim but reflected a profound culture connected to a higher consciousness. Though the ancients may not have achieved as much as modern culture in terms of technology, they possessed a greater awareness of the sacred nature of existence. Their cultures were imbued with religion as a quest for meaning and integration with all life.

My study of the Vedas in the original Sanskrit revealed that Vedic culture was advanced and sophisticated, as much as ancient Egypt or Sumeria. It was a maritime culture that traveled, traded and colonized by sea. It was an urban culture with numerous towns and small kingdoms like classical India. It had a sophistication of arts and crafts, agriculture, science and language. It had a great mythos, a profound ritual and time-honored customs.

The *Rigveda* was a synthetic text produced by a number of different groups over a long period of time and covering a large region of geography. It was the record of a great civilization that found a spiritual unity among the diverse cultures, ethnic and linguistic groups of a vast subcontinent. This is revealed by the many Vedic Gods and Goddesses that each can represent the All as the Supreme Deity as well as having its own unique characteristics. I found the existent history book account of the Aryan invasion, which portrayed the Vedic people as primitive nomads, to be quite erroneous, if not absurd. It had little to do with the Vedic texts and required ignoring or distorting them to fit in with its preconceptions. The term Aryan (*ārya*) in the Vedas has nothing to do with race, language or one group of human beings attacking another. It is a term for good, noble or refined as opposed to those who are evil, ignoble or vulgar. The use of Aryan in a racial sense was an invention of European thinkers steeped in the colonial era and its racist policies.

Civilization all over the world is the product of a commingling of different streams, which is the main Vedic image of life. It comes about through the free interchange of ideas, customs and commodities. It is not the result of some imagined racial or linguistic purity but occurs when people of various backgrounds come together and share their diversity. To try to explain civilization as the product of one race or another is itself racism. To try to explain the development of culture through racial invasions and migrations ignores the creative work of people in the place where they live.

The idea of an Aryan race invading and colonizing India was the shadow of the European colonial model on history that reflected nineteenth century Eurocentric views. It is quite contrary to the Vedic view of many Gods and Goddesses in a wonderful, friendship, harmony and inner unity. Scholars turned mythic wars between the powers of light and darkness into racial wars in India, though the same symbolism occurs throughout ancient civilizations from Egypt to America without such a corresponding human battle.

Such superficial views of ancient teachings, looking at them according to an outer vision of politics and economics has prevented modern scholars from discovering the wealth of spiritual knowledge hidden in such texts. Not only the Vedas but also the *Egyptian Book of the Dead* and Mayan teachings among others have been misread in the same manner.

As a sidelight to my spiritual study of the Vedas, I began putting together an historical view that reflected the spiritual depth that the Vedas had revealed for me. This started as a simple matter of compiling references to the ocean in the *Rigveda* to show that it could not be the product of nomads from Central Asia who never knew of the sea. I was gradually compelled to write a book on Vedic history to counter the existent distortions. I did a first draft in 1980 and gradually developed it further over time. I expanded and finished the work in 1990 and it was published the following year in the United States under the title of *Gods, Sages and Kings: Vedic Secrets of Ancient Civilization.* The book was one of the first titles to raise such issues as the Sarasvati River, Vedic astronomical references and the need for a more consistent rendition of Vedic literature. Little did I know that a great archeological revolution was beginning in India that would verify these views within the next decade.

## Subhash Kak

One of the most notable American Hindus and Vedic scholars that I have known is Subhash Kak. We first began to correspond in 1990 relative to our common interest in ancient India. We met shortly thereafter. Soon we created a close friendship and alliance that has continued throughout the years.

Kak made several brilliant contributions to science in the Vedas, showing the sophistication of mathematics and astronomy that existed at an early era, particularly in the *Śatapatha Brāhmaṇa.* Perhaps most notable is his work unlocking the numerical code behind the organization of the *Rigveda.* He has also made important breakthroughs in deciphering the Indus script. In addition he connected Vedic and Vedantic ideas with the latest insights of modern physics and neuroscience. Along with the noted yoga scholar, Georg Feuerstein, we did a book on ancient India called *In Search of the Cradle of Civilization* that highlighted the new findings on ancient India.

Subhash always emphasized the pursuit of truth, not simply defending a particular religion or culture, however noble it may be. If we are to find value in the Vedas, it is their truth that matters. But the Vedic idea of truth is not just of an objective material order but of cosmic law (*ṛtam*) that imparts harmony to all existence. We must develop that dharmic way of truth and insight, not merely repeat old phrases or uncritically preserve old traditions. The Vedas must be a way to truth or they have no meaning.

## N.S. Rajaram

N.S. Rajaram first wrote me in 1993 in the context of ancient India, an issue that he was beginning to take up. He shortly returned to India from Houston, where he had worked at NASA (National Aeronautics and Space Administration). We exchanged many letters and came to common views and a common plan of action.

Rajaram and I collaborated on several projects, particularly the book *Vedic Aryans and the Origins of Civilization,* which first came out in the Canadian edition in late 1994, with a later India edition through Voice of India. He highlighted my correlation of Vedic literature and Harappan civilization, which is otherwise a literature without a civilization and a civilization without a literature! Later he helped promote the decipherment of the Indus script by Natwar Jha that may unravel the remaining riddles of the ancient Harappan/ Saraswati culture.

Rajaram is a very cogent thinker on modern issues as well as on ancient India. Like myself he was drawn into journalistic role by circumstances, finding how little articulation of a Hindu point of view existed even in India. Having lived in American for twenty years he was not intimidated by the West but had mastered its thinking and its objectivity as well as maintaining his connection to the spiritual culture of India.

Rajaram brought out the information on the Dead Sea Scrolls and modern Biblical scholarship that questioned the historicity and accuracy of the New Testament. While such books are commonly available in the West, they are almost unknown in India, where the average Hindu believes that the Bible is an accurate historical document that has never been tampered with! He also brought to attention in India important critiques about the Vatican well known in the West that reveal the underlying political nature and global aggression of that institution.

## The Birla Science Conference

An important conference on ancient India occurred at the Birla Science Center in Hyderabad in 1994. It featured many leading archaeologists from India including S.R. Rao, S.P. Gupta, Bhagwan Singh, and B.G. Siddharth. All of them emphasized the same theme – that the old Aryan Invasion theory was wrong and went against all existing evidence. A new historical model for ancient India was necessary that showed a greater antiquity and centrality for Vedic culture.

It was encouraging to attend a conference with such eminent archaeologists and scholars and to learn that my work was not just a personal idiosyncrasy but part of a new movement that already had many adherents. The forum was quite heartwarming after the many years of isolated work that I had done. It was clear from the conference that the theory of Aryan Invasion of India was being rejected on all fronts. I was not the only one, nor was my angle of criticism unique. I had merely articulated what many Indians were thinking now and what a number had thought in the past.

## World Association for Vedic Scholars (WAVES)

An alliance of scholars arose in America seeking to promote the new view of ancient India. It gave rise to the World Association of Vedic Studies (WAVES), which held its first conference in Atlanta in October 1996.

James Schaffer of Case Western University, one of the first major Western archaeologists to reject the Aryan Invasion theory, came and spoke. B.B. Lal, one of India's leading archaeologists was there as well, along with many other important speakers and authorities in the field.

A second conference was held in 1998 summer in Los Angeles that continued these activities, which B.B. Lal also attended. There I had an opportunity to get to know Lal better. The leftists had recently targeted Lal as a scholar with a Hindu bias, whose work should therefore be rejected on principle. Lal, however, was a true scholar and archaeologist, relying on objective evidence and years of experience. He was a warm and friendly person with genuine spiritual interests as well as academic objectivity. He was another case of people maligned simply because they were in the way of leftist political interests. However, the leftists were not able to really challenge him on an historical and archaeological basis because his work was solid and rational in its approach.

## Jawaharlal Nehru University (JNU)

The Aryan Invasion issue was a topic that I would lecture on many times in various forums both in India and the United States. It culminated in a lecture that I gave at JNU in Delhi in February 1999. JNU has long been the main center of Marxist thinking in India with many of its prominent professors, like the historian Romila Thapar, being staunch Communists and outspoken defenders of leftist causes. The hall for my lecture was filled with several hundred students, some sitting in the aisles. We had raised the Vedic banner at this prime bastion of Marxism in India for all to see. Along with me were S.P. Gupta, Bhagwan Singh and Devendra Swarup, all notable authorities on ancient India.

The leftist teachers did not challenge our presentation. But a student who was obviously leftist in his views raised a curious question. First he said to my surprise that he accepted our presentation that historical evidence disproved the Aryan

Invasion theory. But, he emphasized, because the demise of the theory would benefit Hindu fundamentalists and their oppressive political agendas, we should continue to uphold this wrong theory anyway in order to prevent a political abuse of history! This reveals the nature of Communist thinking. If the evidence agrees with them they flaunt it. If the evidence goes against them they throw it out. Only politics matters for them in the end.

## Gaining the Ire of Academia

Several academicians, particularly in the West, have criticized my Vedic work, not so much because of the points that I raise but because of my lack of academic qualifications. Since I don't have a degree in Indology from a Western university they hold that anything I say cannot have value and can be rejected without examination. That I have spent many years studying the Vedas and discussing them with traditional teachers doesn't count for them. Few of these scholars have studied the Vedas in the original Sanskrit. Relying on secondhand and outdated sources they often make the most elementary errors in interpretation. The same people reject the views of great yogis like Sri Aurobindo on the Vedas. But they will give credibility to a Communist scholar on the Vedas if he has the appropriate university credentials!

Most academicians refuse to address the issues like the Sarasvati River and the many sites discovered along it. They use the charge of Hindu politics to dismiss any criticism of the Aryan Invasion theory, though colonial, missionary and Marxist groups have long used the theory for their own political gain. Fortunately, a few archaeologists are now rejecting the Invasion theory and other academicians can't so easily ignore them. James Schaffer recently notes:

"As data accumulate to support cultural continuity in south Asian prehistoric and historic periods, a considerable restructuring of existing interpretive paradigms must take place. We reject most strongly the simplistic historical interpretations, which date back to the eighteenth century, that continue to be imposed on South Asian culture history. These still prevailing interpretations are significantly diminished by European ethnocentrism, colonialism, racism, and antisemitism. Surely, as South Asian studies approaches the twenty-first century, it is time to describe emerging data objectively rather than perpetuate interpretations without regard to the data archaeologists have worked so hard to reveal."

'Migration, Philology and South Asian Archaeology' in *Aryan and Non-Aryan in South Asia.*

I learned that the academic realm is not so much a place of objective study as a forum for various vested interests. Academics generally have little respect for spiritual traditions. They assume authority for spiritual subjects beyond their intellectual capacity. They use their positions to further their own political and cultural agendas, often unaware of what they themselves are doing!

In American schools, religions like Hinduism, if they are examined at all, are dissected from a social, political or economic angle as mere cultural phenomena. There is little direct study, much less experience of the Yogic and Vedantic teachings behind the tradition. Such is our modern preoccupation with the outer aspect of life that it reduces spirituality to a purely external affair. No wonder we don't give much credit to a spiritual culture like India.

## The Vedic Yoga

I could easily discern the Vedic roots of the Yoga tradition, its way of mantra and meditation and its understanding of the subtle body and the energies of consciousness. Aurobindo's insights in this direction were a great help. I was only following a path that he had already opened out. However, I was astounded that few scholars had noticed it, even from India. For example, Radhakrishnan missed the boat on the Vedas, even though he knew Aurobindo directly. He preferred the views of Max Müller!

That the Rigvedic deities are symbols of internal processes

was self-evident to me. The Vedic fire on an inner level is the fire of consciousness, *chidāgni*. The Vedic Soma is the Ananda or Bliss. Indra is the Supreme Purusha or pure being and truth, *sat* or *satya*. Vedic mantras reflect the unfoldment of these principles on different planes and levels of the universe, outwardly and inwardly.

For example, Agni or fire on a physical level is the digestive fire. On the vital level it is the fire of *prāṇa* or breath. On the mental level it is the fire of perception. In the *buddhi* or higher mind it is the flame of discrimination (*viveka*). On the spiritual plane it is the flame of awareness.

The Vedas don't project these teachings in an evident but in a cryptic language. They repeatedly say "*paroksha priyā hi devāḥ, pratyaksha dvishaḥ*," meaning "the gods or sages prefer what is indirect and dislike the obvious." The Rishis speak in paradoxes not in evident logic. Such has been the way of many mystics throughout history to take us beyond the outer mind and its limitations.

The *Rigveda* sets forth a path of *mantra yoga*, using sound and the Divine word to awaken our soul. The *Yajurveda* sets forth a path of *prāṇa yoga*, using breath and intention to motivate us inwardly. The *Sāmaveda* sets forth a path of meditation (*dhyāna yoga*), using a heightened state of feeling and awareness to liberate the mind and heart. These three Vedas relate to the three parts of our nature as speech (*vāk*), *prāṇa* and mind (*manas*) and the three states of consciousness as waking, dream and deep sleep. Outwardly they are the three worlds of earth, atmosphere and heaven.

This Vedic path involves both *bhakti* or devotion to the deities as well as *jñāna* or knowledge, understanding the nature of the deities which are all powers of the Self. It set forth the prototype for the entire Hindu tradition and its many sides and approaches.

My earlier Vedic work, particularly my translations from the *Rigveda* as in *Wisdom of the Ancient Seers*, approaches the Vedas but in a deeper philosophical and poetic manner. Today I would explicate these Vedic mantras in a more precise and almost scientific manner, as blueprints of cosmic and psychic forces. This I intend to do in the coming years.

## The Vedic Samaj

Subhash Kak and I developed the idea for a new Vedic association called the Vedic Samaj in 1998. We felt that what is necessary today is not a new religion or even a new guru but a new way of spiritual knowledge and, most importantly, a new type of community to embody it. The Vedic Samaj (Sanātana Vedic Sangha) proposes such a community to celebrate and advance Vedic Dharma in all of its aspects. Such Vedic schools and associations are crucial for a new age of consciousness.

### Purpose of the Vedic Samaj

1. To promote the different systems of Vedic knowledge.
2. To seek the integration of the systems of Vedic knowledge with all valid systems of knowledge, both scientific and spiritual.
3. To provide a way of self-actualization, compassion, and self-fulfillment.
4. To promote harmonious relationships among people and with nature.
5. To develop insight and wisdom for guidance in the unfolding age of information and knowledge.

### Principles of the Vedic Samaj

1. There exists an all-pervasive Supreme Being (*Brahman*) who is both immanent and transcendent.
2. Only through knowing *Brahman* can we reach the goal of life.
3. Spiritually awakened knowledge is essential to know *Brahman*.

4. Knowledge is possible because of the equivalences (*bandhu*) between the outer and the inner. These *bandhus* are described in the Vedas and the Agamas.

5. Yoga, meditation, service, ritual and science are ways to discover knowledge.

6. A Samaj or association is necessary to promote this knowledge and its discovery among people.

7. The Samaj has as its primary principle the seeking of this supreme knowledge, along with the practices and disciplines necessary to bring it about.

8. Membership in the Samaj is based upon personal dedication to the knowledge, its realization and its propagation.

9. The members of the Samaj should meet regularly for worship, meditation and discussion.

# Hindu Groups in the West

Parallel to my work in India I began working with Hindu groups in the United States. Though very few Hindus were living in America when I first began to study Yoga in the late sixties, by the early nineties during which my Vedic work blossomed, they had already become a significant community, highly educated and affluent. In time I visited major Hindu temples and associations throughout the country, particularly in Boston, Houston, and Atlanta. Most important in this regard was the VHP (Vishva Hindu Parishad) of America, but I worked with many other groups as well.

Like their Indian counterpart, the American VHP created a forum for teaching Hinduism, information for defending Hinduism, and communication between various Hindu groups and teachers. I got to know the VHP leaders as well, who have a similar dynamism, intelligence and dedication. It is curious how an organization with such liberal attitudes about life and a broad acceptance of many spiritual paths becomes denigrated as Hindu fundamentalists. Such is the power of propaganda deriving from the need to convert or conquer the world.

I saw many Westernized or American Hindus struggling to rediscover their heritage and make it meaningful for their children. Most were doctors, scientists or in the computer field. Few felt any contradiction between Hindu Dharma and modern science or between being a good Hindu and a good American citizen. In fact I found that Non-resident Indians (NRIs) were more supportive of their Hindu tradition than Hindus in India, particularly those living in big cities or working in the media.

The experience of Western culture had not caused them to abandon their spiritual culture but in the long run brought them back to it. While they appreciate the freedom and affluence of the West they see its spiritual poverty. They also see that Hinduism, particularly through Vedanta, is a much more logical, scientific and futuristic system than Western religions, which even in America have many groups that still espouse the Biblical view of creation with the world starting only 6000 years ago!

The main problem for American Hindus is getting their children, who were born and raised in the West, to understand and respect their tradition. Western pop culture is insidious for getting into the minds of children and turning them toward a lifetime of consumerism, blotting out their finer sensitivities. Still I think if there is any religion that is diverse and rich enough in culture to overcome modern American consumerism, it is the Hindu religion!

## Hindu Students Council

Perhaps the most dynamic group that I met with is HSC or Hindu Students Council. HSC is an organization composed of students and ex-students that promotes Hindu culture, values and ideas on college campuses. It is the largest such organization in the United States, with many branches and hundreds of members. I attended a number of their functions, including those at universities and their summer camps, and got to know many of their leaders.

HSC members have set up the Hindu Universe (www.hindunet.org) which is the largest Hindu internet site. It is an important treasure house of information on all aspects of Hindu religion, thought, culture, history, temples, deities, bhajans et al. They put some of my books and articles on line, as well as those of various Hindu thinkers.

HSC members combine Hindu values, both spiritual and political, with success in the Western business and the academic worlds. They realize that their Hindu background of strong family values, spiritual principles, and dedicated study, affords them an advantage in America. Hinduism is not a liability but an asset to success in the modern world, particularly for the planetary age in which we must go beyond cultural and religious exclusivity. HSC has many brilliant and dynamic young men and women. They will make great contributions to Hinduism in the future and make it more acceptable in the modern world. HSC has a loose association with VHP of America.

## Global Vision 2000

Global Vision 2000 was one of the most important Hindu events ever to occur in the United States. It occurred in 1993 as part of the Vivekananda Centenary celebrations. Many Hindu groups came under the auspices of the VHP. Probably over ten thousand people attended a conference that covered all aspects of Hinduism, India and interreligious dialogue, with programs for the youth as well as adults. I spoke in several sessions and was able to meet many important people. At this gathering one had the sense of a real Hindu community and Hindu voice emerging in the West.

Not surprisingly the media, both Western and Indian, greeted the conference with contempt. They highlight a handful of protestors on the outside and didn't examine the wealth of presentations on the inside, which included Sufi and Native American activities. I have often wondered why other groups are so afraid of Hindus, who are generally tolerant and pacifistic, organizing themselves. I think it is because Hinduism has such a strong culture and teaching that on a level playing field they couldn't compete against it!

## The Swami Narayan Order

The Swami Narayan order is probably the best organized Hindu sect, as well as the most modern in its technology and media resources. At the same time it is probably the best disciplined and the most ascetic of modern Hindu monastic orders.

I was first invited by the Swami Narayan order to their Cultural Festival of India in New Jersey in 1991, to speak before the youth, a role that I would come to take in many different forums. One of the young monks had read my "Arise Arjuna" article and on the pretext invited me. There I had the darshan of Pramukh Swami, their current head and a great Sadhu. Later I visited their temple in India at Akshar Dham in Gujarat where I spoke at a conference on the Role of the Guru. I also visited their beautiful marble temple in London (Neasdon) during a trip to UK.

Most important was my visit to their Cultural Festival of India in 1997 in Mumbai, which marked Pramukh Swami's seventy-fifth birthday, on which occasion I gave a short talk. The Swami Narayan Order had taken a piece of land in the slums of Mumbai and turned it into a modern temple and garden complex showing a futuristic Hinduism with the power to solve all the world's problems. Such is the power of real devotion.

## Tour of UK

In late1996 I did a three week tour of England, speaking at various temples and universities from Newcastle in the North to London in the south and Cardiff in the west. The tour was arranged by the VHP of UK and by the NHSF (National Student's Hindu Forum). They had asked me to release their new book *Explaining Hindu Dharma, a Guide to Teachers*, which had been accepted as a textbook in the British schools.

Like members of HSC, the Hindu students in England were quite enthusiastic and asked many questions on a variety of topics. Hindus in England were a larger portion of the populace and not so spread out as in America. Like their counterparts in America they were affluent and well-educated. However, they were more under siege from

Islamic extremism, which served to give them a greater cohesion.

Most UK Hindus wanted to be called Hindus, unlike most American Hindus who would rather be called Indians or South Asians. As many UK Hindus first came as refugees from British Africa, so that they couldn't be called Indians anyway. The problem was that the appellation South Asian lumped Hindus and Muslims of the subcontinent together, when their culture, educational achievements and role in the UK community are very different. Hindus were high achievers in education, while the Muslims were more inclined to get involved in youth gangs. Hindus did not want to be lumped as South Asians, which would give their merit to the Muslims and ascribe Islamic violence to them.

It was interesting to see India having a reciprocal influence on Great Britain, its former colonial rulers. The British have turned to Indian food. The Hindu religion may gradually come into their lives as well. Certainly the British are much more aware of it than are Americans who often don't know the difference between Hindu and Buddhist, or even Hindu and Muslim

**Trinidad**

One small country in the Americas that does have a large Hindu population is Trinidad. I visited the Island in 1996 and saw its Hindu culture, including its several wonderful temples. It is much like being in India. Even Hindu Gods like Shiva and Hanuman have taken their abode there.

Later I came in contact with the Trinidad Mahasabha that has produced several good writers on Hinduism that write regular articles on topical matters. They asked me never to forget the overseas Hindus in the Caribbean, so I must mention them here as well. There is another large Hindu pocket in Guyana. The Caribbean Hindus show how Hinduism can be adapted to another continent and its landscape. Certainly Hindus have not been properly considerate of their overseas members, which makes them prey to conversion efforts.

The Diaspora of Hindus globally is now quite large, extending to over ten million, and growing rapidly. Often in a foreign context one appreciates one's background better. Hindus are generally more aware of their Hinduness outside of India. That they are targeted by missionaries makes them more conscious of it.

I noted that Hindus do better outside of India, excelling in education and in business. Their very Hindu values of family and learning help them. So it is not Hinduism that makes India poor and inefficient, but the bureaucracy, whose origin is in the British system and in Nehru's adoption of a Soviet style economy. As India comes more under Hindu political and economic values its economic and education levels will rise dramatically.

# 9

# Additional Studies
# of Christianity and Islam

There should be no effort to force any religion upon
anyone. The first commandment of God should be, respect
the Divine Self in all. Secondly there should be no preaching.
We should teach what we know and let others discover for
themselves whether or not it is true. We should let them be
influenced by our behavior and our personality and not resort
to propaganda, threats or promises. We should not speak in
God's name in order to entice or to condemn others. No
religion should make it a right or a duty to convert the world.
We should welcome a diversity of spiritual approaches and
not take any as the last word.

Hindus are not exclusive in their religious, spiritual or
cultural views. They believe in the existence of many paths
both inside their tradition and outside of it. They are ready at
any time to embrace their Christian and Muslim brothers,
without insisting that everyone becomes a Hindu. But one
cannot embrace someone who says, "We do not accept your
religion, we condemn your gods and sages, we reject your
holy books and practices, salvation is ours and not yours, and
we will not cease striving to convert you to our way!" This has
been the main message of Christians and Muslims to Hindus
for centuries, etched in blood, and it remains so today, with a
few notable exceptions and modified according to the
political exigencies of a secular world order.

My main criticism of Christianity and Islam is not about their
beliefs, though I may not agree with these. Let people be

free to follow whatever appeals to them in their hearts. My criticism is against the intolerance and missionary efforts of these two kindred faiths that overshadows the good that they may be otherwise attempting to do.

More liberal Christians may themselves reject such missionary efforts as not representing real Christianity. However, they do little to stop them or even to criticize them. Nor are they aware of how much this missionary aggression still continues. Unless this missionary assault is challenged it is bound to wreak much more havoc in the world, particularly as large Asian countries like China and India become more accessible targets.

Similarly, many Hindus discriminate between churchianity that they reject and Christ whom they honor as a holy man or even avatar. Unfortunately, churchianity still dominates mainstream Christianity and most of Christianity in India as well. The openhearted Hindu acceptance of Christ has even been used by missionaries to soften up Hindus for their conversion efforts, not by reciprocating with any comparable honoring of Krishna or Buddha.

If Christians and Muslims want to show their tolerance let them first throw off their exclusivism and accept other paths, including the Pagan and Hindu as valid. Let them close down their conversion activities and openly dialogue with other religions to jointly discover what is true. Let them apologize for their history of denigrating other faiths and seeking to convert them with force and propaganda. Otherwise those of other beliefs cannot trust their claims of tolerance.

Many good people and even great mystics have lived among Christians and Muslims throughout history. I would certainly not deny this. All human beings have access to the Divine and Christians and Muslims are not barred from it. The problem is that their exclusive beliefs and their missionary efforts removes them from the Divine in others and causes them to lose the Divine within themselves as well. It makes them try to denigrate and destroy other traditions that are quite valid in their own right.

All human beings possess a natural faith and intuition in a higher truth and consciousness. The problem is that religions, instead of facilitating this, try to manipulate it into a faith in their own dogmas and institutions instead – and an intolerance of other forms that this inner yearning may take among different people and cultures. In this way true religious seeking, which is valid whatever form it takes, becomes distorted and even harmful. It misses its real goal of uniting humanity and becomes a factor of social division and distrust. It suppresses the pursuit of spiritual and even scientific knowledge that it cannot control.

## Islam and the Sufis

As I traveled in India I noticed the Islamic community and how it operates. Islamic women still wear the veil and dark clothing. Muslims stay apart from Hindus in their own communities, which are often ghettos. Clearly there was a major cultural difference between Hindus and Muslims.

I wondered why the Sufis, who follow a mysticism like Ibn El Arabi that has much in common with Vedantic monism, did not project a more positive model of Hinduism for orthodox Muslims to emulate. I researched the Sufis further. I discovered that the Sufis were a diverse group representing various intellectual and mystical trends in the Islamic world, both orthodox and unorthodox. Some Sufis were indeed free spirited individualists with a direct communion with the Divine at a high level. The medieval Persian poet Rumi is perhaps the best example of this type of Sufi. Such Sufis were often oppressed, if not killed by the Muslim orthodoxy, like Al Hallaj in the ninth century, who was dismembered for making the rather Vedantic proclamation of "I am God."

Other Sufis were simply the Islamic equivalent of the Jesuits and could be militant, if not fanatic. Such Sufis encouraged and guided Muslim attacks against Hindu India. This was particularly true of organized Sufi orders like the Naqshbandis, which have long aimed at the conversion of India to Islam. These Sufi orders are spiritual soldiers for

Islam and, like Christian missionaries, have little respect for other traditions, particularly those of India, which they still denigrate as *kāfir*. Most Sufi activity in the world today is under their control.

The other question was whether Mohammed, the founder of Islam, who had many mystical experiences, was a tolerant figure whose teachings were distorted by militant Islam, or an intolerant figure that militant Islam followed faithfully. In the beginning I assumed that Mohammed was probably a great yogi whose teaching was misinterpreted, following a common Hindu idea that all major religions must reflect the highest truth at their origin. However, over time after studying the *Koran* and the life of Mohammed, I was forced to conclude that Islamic intolerance began with Mohammed himself. I came to agree with Swami Vivekananda that Mohammed was an eccentric mystic who mixed various superstitions with an experience of superconsciousness that was incomplete. The result was a dangerous combination of religious insight and religious fanaticism.

I discovered that the majority of Sufis have long been actively engaged in promoting Islamic expansionism and aggression, and this remains part of their agenda today. Prominent Sufis were involved with major Islamic rulers in India, including tyrants like Mahmud Ghaznavi, Mohammed Ghauri, Alauddin Khilji, and Aurangzeb, who killed thousands of Hindus and destroyed hundreds of temples. Mahmud Ghaznavi, for example, was a great hero in the Sufi poetry of Attar and Sanai, for his ruthless destruction of the Somnath Shiva temple, which they saw as a den of infidels.

Perhaps because Islam is generally intolerant, the Sufis gain much by way of contrast. While one can sympathize with the Sufis and more easily dialogue with them than with the orthodox, to think that Sufis don't represent the vested interests of Islam is quite naïve. I remember a meeting with an American Sufi who followed a traditional Middle Eastern Sufi order. He admitted that non-Muslims could gain access to

Allah but insisted that it required a special effort on their part. I mentioned the example of Ramana Maharshi. He noted that the Maharshi's achievement was great for a Hindu but ordinary Muslims could reach the same level without effort by faith alone. He said that through Islam one connects to a lineage that goes all the way back to Adam or the original man and connects one directly with God, while all other religions deviate from that and cannot be trusted!

In my dialogues with various Sufis I found that they didn't accept karma and rebirth. In spite of their portrayal in India as monists, they were generally dualists, seeing some ultimate difference between God and the soul. Though they firmly believe that God is One they feel that the human soul can never completely merge into Allah but can only go to one of the nine heavens or paradises. While many accept a unity of religions, if you question them they usually place that unity only in Islam, not in any real religious pluralism.

## Anwar Shaikh

During my UK trip I met with Anwar Shaikh, an important scholarly critic of Islam. Originally a Pakistani, an Islamic Mullah and a Sufi Sheikh, he returned to the Vedic fold by his own thought and experience. Shaikh was a warm and friendly character with a great sense of humor and hospitality. He was not physically well at the time but was still working hard on various books and articles.

Shaikh has an evolutionary concept of the Godhead, that the Divine was a collective formation of cosmic evolution, not an aloof God outside of the cosmos. This corresponds to the Hiranyagarbha or collective subtle body of Vedantic thought. We are all creating God as God is living through us. Buddhist and Jain ideas of liberation as something that we develop on an individual level rather than as something that comes from a deity beyond reflect a similar trend in Indian thought.

Shaikh regards Islam as a political movement under a

religious guise, a ploy for Arab nationalism. For him Mohammed was a masterful general, politician and diplomat who skillfully used religion to further his worldly aims. Allah is an alter ego for Mohammed and the *Koran* is more the thought and life of Mohammed than a real communion with God. Shaikh has a mastery of Arabic, the *Koran* and its traditional commentaries and uses them to prove his point of view. Another important work in this regard is *Why I Am Not A Muslim* by Ibn Warraq, who also opens the veil of scrutiny on Islam that has been so carefully kept intact by Islamic rulers today.

Islamic mullahs like the Ayatollah Khomeni remind one of fundamentalist Christian preachers in America who repeatedly assert that "God said" or "Jesus said" when they really are just voicing their own opinions and assertions. They use the name of God to promote their social agendas of controlling or expanding their flocks. God certainly has his own voice that can be heard in the heart and has nothing to do with any preaching. We all belong to the community of God. The real sin is to divide humanity into the true believers and the heretics, which leads to hatred and war. And if God demands such exclusive loyalty, such a God is a creation of human need and arrogance, not the universal truth or love. He should not be worshipped but cast aside.

The whole idea of a messenger between God and Man – that the individual cannot directly understand God but requires a prophet or savior like Mohammed or Jesus – is foreign to Hindu thought that emphasizes the Atman or higher Self. One could argue that the setting up of such a messenger is the real idolatry or worship of a false god. It places an intermediary between the soul and God, which is then used by various vested interests to direct our faith not to God, but to their own dogmas and need to control the world. Similarly the Hindu view, while honoring the books of the sages, never puts any holy book as the last word that we must uncritically accept. Our own direct perception of truth is made the highest authority.

Clearly the world needs a more critical examination of Islam, both historically and ideologically. The Islamic world stands where Christianity was in the Middle Ages, preventing anyone from questioning its beliefs in a manner on par with the Inquisition, yet with the economic power of billions of petrodollars. Religion should be objectively examined not only from the light of reason, but also according to a dharmic or yogic view.

Such intellectual critiques were made of Christianity several centuries ago. But Islamic society is not yet open to such self-examination. Though a fatwa and death threat has been issued against him for his views, Anwar Shaikh has invited Muslim scholars to debate freely with him whenever they like. So far no one has taken up his challenge. Even if one does not agree with such critics as Shaikh, there is no reason that their lives should be threatened because they question Islam.

## Visit to Israel

I visited Israel in February of 1995 as part of an international Yoga conference where I was teaching. The trip helped me better understand Western religions. I found Israel to be a fascinating country with a deep and ancient spirit that reflected the formlessness and austerity of the surrounding desert. In some ways it reminded me of South India.

Strangely perhaps, given my Catholic background, the religion that most interested me while in Israel was Judaism, which I felt most acutely while visiting the Wailing Wall. I had long admired the Jewish people for their intellectual achievements and viewed their religion in a different light than Christianity or Islam. Unlike its offshoots, the Jewish religion never set itself up as the one true faith that needed to conquer the world. It accepted that different peoples had other religious traditions, which might not be the same as theirs. It also had great traditions of learning, mysticism and the use of a spiritual language that were almost Brahmanical in nature. Some Jewish groups also accept rebirth or reincarnation.

The *Bible* is mainly the cultural record of the Jewish people, coming from various Jewish leaders over many centuries compiled to deal with the issues of their community, not only spiritual but also mundane. That the *Bible* is the word of God is cultural hyperbole; it represents the Jewish people's main experience and interpretation of the Divine, not God's last word for all humanity or for all time.

I could see how the Jews would think that Christians and Muslims had expropriated and distorted their teaching. The Christians transformed the *Bible* into a teaching that was even used to attack the Jews. The *Koran* is the *Bible* rewritten according to the religious urges of the Arabic community, and reflects their social and political expansion as well. The whole idea of a book as the Word of God moved from cultural pride to global aggression.

At first I couldn't understand why the Jews were opposed to image worship, which most divides their tradition from the Hindu. Images are part of our artistic expression and are helpful tools for devotion. Image worship may not appeal to everyone, but there is no need to exclude it. And it is quite unenlightened to reject all images as unholy or those who worship them as unspiritual.

However, I discovered an historical reason for the Jewish rejection of image worship. The Jews were a small people that occupied an important trade and military route between two continents, which was a natural battleground for nearby empires. With the larger, more elaborate and imagistic Egyptian and Mesopotamian cultures on either side, the Jews could have been easily assimilated. Their aniconic religion aided in their survival by making them a distinct people and helping them stand apart from their often more materialistic neighbors. Unfortunately this social need got translated into a religious rule that became the basis of religious intolerance, particularly under Christian and Islamic dogma.

I also admired the Greek Orthodox churches in Jerusalem, which were quite beautiful and ornate, much like Hindu temples with their images, incense and candles. I learned that the Greek Orthodox tradition is the older form of Christianity. All the old churches in Jerusalem are Greek Orthodox, which was the religion of the Eastern Roman or Byzantine Empire. The Roman Catholics didn't get to Jerusalem until the time of the Crusades and don't represent either original Christianity or its forms near its homeland in Israel, which were more mystical in nature.

However, Christianity in all its forms appeared to be permeated with a sense of sorrow, the crucified savior, and a burden of original sin. I think there is a deeper meaning for this. Christianity reflects a mystical vision that was crushed before it could really develop. From a Jewish religious sect opposing the Romans it eventually assumed the power of the Roman State and came to embody the very tyranny that it first opposed.

A study of the Dead Sea Scrolls reveals that the early Christians were one of many related Jewish movements of the times opposed to the Romans. Most of the teachings attributed to Jesus were part of older Jewish teachings, including many of his parables. These portray a similar symbolism of a Messiah and looking to the end of the world, which really meant the end of Roman rule and the reestablishment of a Jewish state. The Messiah was a purely Jewish concept, not the harbinger of a new faith.

Jesus, if anything, was a good Jew and should be interpreted in light of Jewish traditions. Though he may have opposed certain Jewish sects, which were many, he was clearly in the line of the Old Testament. Christianity was a misinterpretation of Judaism that occurred after the Romans destroyed the Jewish State and killed its leaders, including the early Christians and their leaders like James, called the brother of Jesus. It took several centuries for Jewish Christianity to evolve into Roman Christianity and we can document this historically with the aid of various historical records. Paul was pivotal in turning this Jewish sect into a Roman religion. He was the real founder of the Christian religion not Jesus or his disciples who remained faithful Jews.

Roman Christianity was the invention of a later age when the Jewish Christians, defeated and scattered by the Romans, reorganized and intermingled with the general Roman public. In order to gain support in Roman society they downplayed and then denied their Jewish background. This Roman Christianity that became the official Roman religion in the fourth century was the Greek Orthodox tradition and brought in some of the mysticism and image worship of the Greeks and related Gnostic traditions.

The Roman Catholic religion only became prominent through Charlemagne and the Holy Roman Empire in the ninth century. Roman Catholic Christianity with its popes was a sidelight to Greek Orthodox Christianity that only came to dominate over the Greek tradition after the Crusades that sacked the Greek capital of Byzantium in the thirteenth century.

In Jerusalem I could see a decline in spirituality from the Greek Orthodox to the Roman Catholic churches and Protestant churches. The Greek Orthodox churches had much mysticism in them. The Roman Catholic had some mysticism but a sense of regimentation. The recently built Protestant churches had no spirituality at all and were little better than tombs for the soul!

Scholars are now discovering a similar historical development in the *Koran*. Versions of the *Koran* from Yemen have been found dating from the eighth century that differ from the *Koran* as we know it today. Scholars are now proposing that the *Koran* was a document that developed over time to fulfill not only religious needs but also the social needs of a new and rapidly growing empire. The new Arab rulers needed a religious teaching to sanctify their position and maintain their hold over the older and more complex cultures that they had just come to rule. Their religion was rigid and intolerant in order to sustain their supremacy over older civilizations that could easily assimilate their much simpler culture.

No doubt many mystical traditions existed in the ancient Near East (West Asia) before the two orthodox religions of the book eliminated them. This included Greek, Celtic, Egyptian, Persian and Babylonian traditions with probable links to India and to Vedanta. Probably there were many great mystics in these traditions that we have forgotten who were as great as any produced by Christianity and Islam.

## Vedic Pluralism and Biblical Monotheism

Biblical traditions reflect a One God who is an authoritarian figure, having his chosen people, demanding allegiance, exhibiting jealousy, and lording over his creation like a king, if not a tyrant. While some may argue that this is a misinterpretation or a simplification of a deeper view, and it may be, it has been the dominant impulse behind missionary efforts all over the world. In the Christian view God has his heaven and hell to reward his followers and punish his enemies. Islam follows the same model. Such a God is looked upon with fear and trembling. His believers follow him as a role model and easily become intolerant and authoritarian themselves, asserting dogma rather than seeking truth, trying to make everyone follow the dictates of their imperious deity.

The Vedic view, on the contrary, is of many Gods and Goddesses, each with its appropriate and unique place in the cosmic order. Behind them is not some domineering personal Creator but a Great Spirit or Parabrahma, which is our higher Self beyond all outer limitations. The Vedic Gods form a vast and friendly brotherhood and work together to manifest the Great Spirit. While some like Rudra are figures of some fear or dread, representing difficult aspects of life such as death and suffering, even these can be propitiated and turned into benefic forces of light and love. Perhaps the Old Testament

God was originally such a Rudra-Shiva like figure that got scaled down into a more limited or exclusive model over time. Rudra is also called *yahva* in the *Rigveda*, perhaps cognate with the Biblical Yahweh.

In the Biblical tradition human beings are fallen creatures, existing in sin and exiled from God, who stands with a threatening gaze in his heaven beyond. In the Vedas, human beings form a brotherhood with the Gods and have a common origin, nature and kinship with them. Human beings can become Gods and gain immortality along with them. There is no overriding or ultimate sin but simply ignorance and impurity that must be removed to allow our true nature, which is pure awareness, to manifest without obstruction.

Biblical monotheism tends towards exclusivism – if you are not with us, you are against us. The Vedic view reflects unity-in-multiplicity – those who sincerely think differently than us are also with us, because there is no one way for all. The Vedic view is of a pluralistic world order that accommodates many variant views in a vast harmony. It is aware of the Absolute Unity of Truth but also recognizes its many creative forms in manifestation.

The main Biblical view is that "I, the Lord thy God, am a jealous God and thou shall not worship other Gods." The Vedic view is "That which is the One Truth the Seers declare in manifold ways (*Rigveda* I.164.46)", and "May noble aspirations come to us from every side (*Rigveda* I.89.1)." The Rigvedic original man or Manu states, "None of you Gods are small or inferior. All of you are great. All the Gods that dwell here, who are universal to all beings, may you give your protection to us and to our horses and cattle (*Rigveda* VIII.30.1,4)."

The Biblical view is of a One God who is at war with other gods. The Vedic view is of One Truth that has many forms, expressions and paths of approach. Whether it is Indra, Agni, Soma and Surya of the Vedas or Shiva, Vishnu, Devi or Ganesha of later Hinduism, each is the Supreme Self in form, aspect or approach and includes the other Gods in a greater harmony.

Vedic pluralism gives rise to a free and open spiritual path, the many ways of yoga. It is not limited to monotheism, though it includes theism as an important approach at a devotional level. Vedic pluralism does not give rise to any need to convert the world but rather to the nurturing of ever new insights and local applications of truth. Nor is it a form of polytheism, reflecting a belief in many separate gods. It is a free approach to monism on an individual level, recognizing both the universal and the unique in human beings. Such a view is necessary today to link all the varied religious aspirations of humanity and the many sages, teachings and forms of worship that are our heritage as a species.

The Hindu way is a universal pluralism that combines the one and the many, the unique and the all. It is not a pluralism of anything goes, a mere promiscuity, but a truth that is vast, many sided and adaptable, like the great forces of nature. It is the pluralism that arises from the One, but the One that is infinite and unlimited. Such an inclusive view is necessary to integrate human culture throughout the world today, which is and should remain diverse. The exclusivist model belongs to the Middle Ages and reflects the urge of one group to triumph over the rest, which leads to conflict and destruction.

Hinduism does not claim to hold the big or the final truth, or to dispense it to a doubting humanity from on high. It holds that a Supreme Truth, a unity of consciousness, does exist but that it is beyond human manipulation and outside of human history. This spiritual truth has nothing to do with proselytizing and is not bound by any belief, identity or leader. Discovering it is ultimately a matter of individual search and aspiration. Hinduism provides tools for this self-discovery, but leaves the individual free to find out directly what it is. As a religion it makes itself dispensable and does not make itself into the last word. Once we know ourselves we go beyond all the limitations of humanity. But at the same time we become connected to all the great seers and yogis of all time.

## Religion and Superstition

Religion is inherently an attempt to connect with the transcendent. Such a connection not only enlarges human consciousness but, if done without the right purity of body and mind, can expand the human ego instead. It can not only connect us with the Absolute but can lend the illusion of absolute truth to our own prejudices.

The Hindu tradition emphasizes yogic *sādhanā* to purify the body and mind so that we have the proper vessel to experience superconsciousness. But religious teachings that emphasize faith and belief do not require such *sādhanā*. Faith-based religions encourage belief in the irrational like the virgin birth or redemption on the cross as necessary for salvation, not changing one's own consciousness. This placing of faith beyond scrutiny tends to imbalance the minds of people and makes them prone to wishful thinking and emotional excesses.

Mysticism can exist within the confines of religious dogma but inevitably gets distorted by it. Even when people have genuine experiences of higher states of consciousness in belief-based traditions, like many Christian mystics, the dogmas and superstitions of their religions cast a shadow over these. Some such mystics may get caught in delusions, thinking that they are another Jesus or that they are at war with the devil and have to save the world. The mystification of salvation through belief in a savior or prophet leads to much confusion and is incapable of really changing human nature. This is because the impure mind mixes its own desires with any experience of the Divine that it may be able to achieve.

The Vedic tradition, on the other hand, emphasizes the impersonal (*apaurusheya*) and the eternal (*sanātana*). It is not rooted in an historical revelation but in an ever-evolving quest for truth. It recognizes both many ancient and many modern sages and the individual's need for direct perception. Religions rooted in the personal and historical (*paurusheya*) tend to confuse the merely human with the Divine. They invest an infallibility to certain prophets, books or institutions, which existing in time must be fallible. They confuse promoting a human religious identity with the search for truth within their own minds and hearts. They remain trapped in the needs of a particular community and frozen at one stage of history.

Books like the *Bible* and the *Koran* are human inventions and contain much that is untrue or out of date. They may represent how certain people tried to connect with the divine, but they do not represent the Divine itself. They are not of universal or eternal relevance but have a niche in time and space that can be quite limiting. Even the Vedas are not literally the word of God, which is beyond all form, but the spiritual records of the Rishis and the various ways that they sought the Divine. We should never worship a mere book. A book can only be an aid for our own inner inquiry, just as a guidebook can never substitute for our own travel to a new country. That is why we are told that the Vedas are endless. Truth is beyond limitation. The unspoken word or unstruck sound is greater than what anyone may ever say.

Religion in the world today still promotes many superstitions, not merely about the world, but also about the nature of consciousness. I am not speaking only of tribal beliefs but also of mainstream faiths. If we look at all the claims of salvation in religion, they remain naïve, if not absurd. The necessity for Jesus as our personal savior, or Mohammed as the last prophet, are contrary to both reason and to spiritual wisdom. Knowledge alone brings liberation and it comes not through belief but through meditation.

We need not accept all these religious superstitions in order to be liberal in our religious views but should cut through them with the light of discrimination. Truth arises through self-discovery, which requires going beyond all prophets and intermediaries. In this regard truth is more important than God. Our real search should be for truth. That will lead us to the real divinity. But if we seek God according to the idea of a certain faith, we are likely to lose the truth along the way.

# 10

# Return of the Pagans

Once human beings communed freely with the forces of nature. They felt a spirit in every hill or vale. They saw a Divine face in the Sun and the Moon. They felt a consciousness in the mountains, trees and clouds. They recited poetry, performed rituals, and had profound meditations on the sacred world order, which they discovered allied with their own inner Self. Those who possessed such insight were the sages, seers, druids or rishis that guided the culture.

The advent of the One God and his One Book banished the nature spirits from the Earth, disconnected us from our ancestors, and removed us from the grace of the great Gods and Goddesses. Our human god like a superego came to rule over our psyche and alienate us from life. Pagan learning that included natural healing, astrology, the occult and yoga was dismissed as dangerous, if not demonic.

This One God was not a universal formation (though one may argue that he originally might have been). He represented not a unity of truth, but a single God opposed to all others. He demands, like a jealous husband, an exclusive loyalty. He brought his people not to the Oneness but to a duality of the true believer and the infidel that ushered in a reign of mistrust, hatred and eventually terror upon the world in the name of religion.

But the One God could only rule over a dark age of the oppression. He had to banish the light of reason and freedom of inquiry, maintaining his rule with force and propaganda. His rule, though lasting for some centuries, had to be transient. With the return of reason, observation and open communication in the modern world, his domination must come to an end. The great Gods and Goddesses are again returning as our natural interest in higher consciousness reawakens. May their beautiful and friendly grace come forth once more!

## Hinduism and Native Traditions

Hinduism reflects the religion of nature and the earth. It is present externally in the clouds and the stars, the hills and the rivers. We can see Hinduism in all native traditions and in all ancient religions, particularly where the Sun, the symbol of the Atman or higher Self, is worshipped. Hindu Dharma is the very religion of life and of the individual expressing himself or herself in many different forms.

Encountering Hinduism is particularly difficult because it means facing our Pagan roots. Were the Pagans really that bad? Were they merely bloodthirsty savages as we generally portray them to be? Did only Christianity bring civilization and compassion to the world? Were the Pagans, even if great, doomed to hell or at least to inadequacy because of not accepting Jesus, though most of them never heard of him?

I cannot believe that our ancient ancestors were so inferior or that we are so much more advanced. I don't think that merely embracing a religious belief really changes people or makes them better. Our Pagan ancestors were human beings with a profound sense of the sacred. Could they not also feel the full range of emotions up to communion with God? Our words God and Divine, after all, are Pagan in origin. Certainly the Pagans knew of a higher power and had methods to connect with it. They had deep spiritual traditions abounding with holy places, myths, philosophy, magic and insight.

The Pagans were tolerant about religion and delighted in a variety of teachings, ever welcome to embrace new Gods and Goddesses. We find a great diversity of religious practices in native religions, whether in Europe, the Near

East or in Asia. Christianity reduced these practices, not by understanding them but by summarily rejecting them, because they were too diverse for its monotonous creed.

Have those of you who came from Christian or Islamic religious backgrounds ever asked what the religion of your ancestors was before they converted? Was their religion mere idolatry, superstition, and eroticism as Paganism is portrayed to be? Or did it have its own nobility and spirituality, its own sense of the Divine and a great history and ancestry? We can better understand these older beliefs because their counterpart exists in native traditions throughout the world, above all in India.

Native religions are not credal beliefs based upon a church, scripture or prophet. They are rooted in the land and in the sky, not in a book or in an institution. They are part of a people, culture and way of life. While some of their beliefs may appear primitive or crude to our casual glance, we can find great meaning in them if we would but look upon them with sensitivity and openness.

We should remember the example of the Native Americans who suffered deception and genocide by the expanding Christian Europeans. The natives honored all treaties, but the White Men, the so-called civilized and religious people, broke them all in their greed for land and wealth. They herded the natives like cattle, split up their families, tore them off the land that was their soul, and placed them in reservations that were little better than prisons. And, most strangely, they thought in this cruel process that they were actually civilizing the natives and giving them the chance to become good Christians!

The pre-Christian Greeks gave us Plato and Aristotle or Western philosophy, on which mooring later Christian theology, without much appreciation, built its foundations. They gave us a great mythology full of deep and complex meanings with their great Gods and Goddesses from Zeus to Apollo, from Aphrodite to Hera. Great ancient European mystics like Plotinus or Apollonius of Tyna were not Christians and didn't require a church or a book to mediate between themselves and the Infinite. And they looked to India for inspiration not to the *Bible*.

The Celts had their bards and seers; the famous Druids that even the inimical Romans looked to as wise and noble. The Druids had an oral tradition of poetry, along with rituals or *yajñas* much like the Vedas. They knew the land and its spirits, the mists and the hills. They had their medicine, astrology and philosophy. The Egyptians gave us great pyramids and a monumental artwork that reflects cosmic consciousness and a profound knowledge of the occult. Even today we are in awe of their accomplishments and cannot reduplicate them.

It is the very nature of credal religions to denigrate, if not demonize different beliefs. For example, the Muslims of the Middle Ages prided themselves in destroying the idols of the evil pagans. Their word for idol was Bud for Buddha. The people they vilified as the terrible and hedonistic pagans were often merely pacifistic Buddhist monks!

## Christian Oppression of Pagans

In my studies of history I learned that the Pagan oppression of the Christians was minor compared to the Christian oppression of Pagans. Pagan Rome was generally tolerant about religion and accepted the existence of many cults and sects. Its clash with Christianity was because the Christians refused to afford homage to the Roman State. No doubt the Romans, who were harsh rulers of a vast empire, did oppress the early Christians. But the many religions in the Roman Empire had great depths and cannot be rejected for this political action.

In the early centuries of Christian rule numerous Pagan temples were destroyed or replaced by churches. Their beautiful statues were broken and trampled upon as unholy idols. Their wonderful rituals and philosophies were rejected as superstition. The great university and library of Alexandria was only one of the many centers of learning in the ancient world that was destroyed. Eventually the Platonic Academy in Athens was closed down as well. Early Christianity was against learning and burned books and schools, a model that early Islam also followed.

Some Pagan beliefs were taken over by the Church like Christmas, which was originally a Mithraic winter solstice festival, or the Christmas tree, which was a Pagan German custom. The Madonna was adopted from the old Pagan Goddesses. Some of the most charming and mystical aspects of Christianity were originally Pagan!

Note how negative in connotation the term pagan is today, even though so much was taken from them. This reflects deep-seated religious prejudices. The same negative meanings are given to the term Hinduism as well, which connotes the worst of paganism to the modern mind.

This authoritarianism of credal beliefs caused them to suppress their own mystics as well. The Church oppressed Christian mystics and orthodox Mullahs oppressed Islamic sufis. A Christian mystic like St. Francis of Assisi is at least half a Pagan. His Brother Sun and Sister Moon is but an echo of the Pagan Father Sun and Mother Moon or Divine Father and Divine Mother! His song needs to be finished.

Clearly native beliefs are not unspiritual. There is more of real mysticism in them than in the credal beliefs that have so long been seeking to displace them. Mainstream Christianity and Islam are afraid of mysticism and against the occult. They don't like gurus and are wary of anyone who thinks that he can have a direct experience of God apart from their one savior or final prophet.

What the Christians did in the Americas continued a policy of oppression that began centuries before in Europe. It was not being Western or European that created this religious intolerance but the kind of exclusive belief system that mainstream Christianity and Islam followed. Pre-Christian

Europeans like the Celts had more in common with the Native Americans than with the Europeans colonists who conquered them. The Celts themselves were earlier victims of the same aggression that the Native Americans had to face.

Hindu Dharma never sought to displace native traditions but has honored them and tried to harmonise with them. It is a natural friend of Pagan and native traditions everywhere. One does not have to give up one's ancestry or deny one's native culture in order to embrace Hindu Dharma. One simply has to be willing to honor all spiritual approaches, along with freedom and diversity in the spiritual realm.

The Hindu tradition honors the Goddess, who is important in all Pagan traditions and was generally rejected by the Biblical traditions. It has preserved all the forms of the Great Goddess from the Earth Mother to the Sky Goddess, from the Great Mother to the woman warrior. All those seeking to restore the Goddess religion will find much of value in Hinduism, which has preserved the full range of human spiritual aspiration.

## Becoming a Pagan

This pursuit of finding one's own dharma drew me to examine the pre-Christian traditions of Europe, notably the Celtic traditions from which my Irish ancestors derived. I don't see any contradiction between their traditions and Hinduism. Fortunately, the core of their traditions has survived the many centuries of oppression and is flowering anew. With time and help from other native traditions, they may yet reclaim their full glory and splendor.

Starting in 1996 I came into a contact with Celtic groups and began to discuss issues of history and religion with them. Most of them honor Hinduism and feel a kinship with it. They are looking to Hindu India as a new model of resurgent Paganism in the world. They are discovering in the Hindu tradition for what has been lost in their own traditions.

In contact with my Celtic friends and by their advice this year (1999) I reclaimed my Irish family line for the Celtic religion and its Vedic connections. While I am not specifically doing Celtic practices, I have added a Celtic slant on my Hindu practices. One can see Lord Shiva in the Celtic God Cernunos, who is also the Lord of the Animals, Pashupati. The Celtic Green Man shows the Purusha or Divine Spirit in nature, which in plants is the Vedic God Soma. In time I hope to incorporate a greater understanding of the Celtic ways into my work and into my communion with nature.

This revival of native religions is gaining ground worldwide and is bound to become much more significant in the future. Major conferences of Pagan, native or ethnic religions are occurring to coordinate this interest. The Catholic Church in Europe now sees neo-Paganism as a real threat to its survival. It has tried for two thousand years to eliminate Paganism and has not succeeded. This is because the Pagan traditions reflect integral aspects of our eternal spirituality that can never be eliminated, any more than we can live without breathing.

Such neo-Pagan movements exist throughout Europe and America. They are complemented by a revived interest in Native American, Native African, Hawaiian, and Australian traditions. All these groups are discovering an affinity with Hinduism. Hinduism as the best surviving of the Pagan or native traditions gives a sense of their great depth and power. Hindu Dharma can be an excellent friend and ally in reclaiming and reuniting all native traditions, which still suffer much oppression and remain under siege by missionary influences.

May the Pagans return, along with their many Gods and Goddesses, free to reintegrate the Earth once more with the Divine, without any church or dogma to prevent them!

# 11

## Debate with the Archbishop
## of Hyderabad on the Conversions Issue

In late 1998 a Hindu backlash occurred against the Christian conversion effort in India. This happened mainly in tribal communities that had long been targeted by the missionaries. Note that Christian missionaries don't come to dialogue with Hindu religious leaders, whom they cannot possibly convert, but to target the poor and uneducated. What does this say about their motives?

Rather than looking to the real cause of the problem, which was missionary interference in tribal life, the Western influenced media tried to blame Hindu fundamentalism as the danger. They portrayed Hindus as intolerant and exaggerated the violence against Christians while ignoring Christian violence against Hindus. They failed to remember the bloody history and intolerant attitudes of the missionaries. Though only one missionary was killed during the entire period, they tried to portray it as a bloodbath or massacre of Christians in India.

In response the Prime Minister of India, Atal Behari Vajpayee, asked for a national debate on the conversion issue. Prajna Bharati of Hyderabad, an important Hindu organization, asked me to participate in this national issue by debating with Archbishop Arulappa of Hyderabad, who at the age of seventy-six was the seniormost Catholic monk in India. This was quite a challenge! I had to be a spokesperson for Hindu Dharma in a major public forum, with one of India's foremost Christian leaders, educated at Oxford, who had much international experience as a teacher and speaker. The Archbishop read off a prepared statement, highlighting the need for religious tolerance and peace in the world, such as no one could object to, while emphasizing India's history of pluralism and tolerance in religious matters. However, he failed to address the conversion issue directly or the dangers caused by proselytizing both historically and today. I also had prepared a speech to read but set it aside and spoke extemporaneously.

In the question and answer period the Archbishop surprisingly made a strong statement about the dangers of proselytizing, which was shocking to other Christians in India. Unfortunately, no other Christian leaders in India, much less in the rest of the world echoed such statements, which are not part of Church policy. Some of his relevant statements in this regard are quoted below:

"Conversion has no meaning! Proselytisation has no meaning if you do not convert yourself to God and see what God has to tell you. Follow his will, his plan and that is real religion. So therefore, I personally do not believe at all in proselytisation.

The last point I would like to say is that, Christianity has made terrible blunders in the past! Terrible, not horrible! One of them was to mix faith with culture. If you go to India, you take Indian culture, if you go to Africa, take African culture, if you go to Japan, take Japan culture. We have made a lot of mistakes, a lot of blunders. That there is no salvation outside of Christ is not fully true. It is one way of looking at it if we have faith. But what I said was, salvation is from God, not from religion. If you understand that fully, the full answer is there."

I have included the relevant portions of my speech. For those wanting the full text and the Archbishop's statements, please contact Prajna Bharati.

## Speech at Prajna Bharati

*Delivered at a public discussion organised by Prajna Bharati, A.P., on "The Ethics of Religious Conversions" on February 9, 1999 at Bharatiya Vidya Bhavan, Hyderabad.*

I was raised as a Catholic and went to Catholic school. My uncle was, and still is, a missionary. We were told that he was going to South America to save the souls of the Native Americans, people we were told were non-Christian and without conversion would suffer eternal damnation. This is the background that I came from.

Today, throughout the world, and in the United States, with very little exception, there is no "*sarvadharma-samabhāva*" taught in religion. It is something I never encountered in my Christian education in the West.

We were taught that Hinduism was a religion of idolatry; it was a religion of polytheism and superstition and that there was no place for Hindus in heaven. Even a great Hindu like Mahatma Gandhi might be revered on a certain level, but he was not given the type of religious credit that he would have been given had he been a Christian.

These attitudes still exist throughout the world and India does not exist in isolation. And Hindus in India are, and India as a whole is, still being targeted for conversion. Why is this so? If all the religions teach the same thing, why is it that certain religions are seeking to convert the members of other religions to their beliefs?

Hinduism is a pluralistic tradition. It teaches that there are many paths, many scriptures, many sages, many ways to come to the Divine to gain self-realization and it should be free for the individual to find and follow whatever way he or she thinks or feels works best.

But not all religions are pluralistic. In fact, most religions are exclusive in their mentality and in their beliefs. The two largest religions in the world, with a few notable exceptions, teach that theirs is the only true faith. The average Christian throughout the world has been taught to believe that only Christians gain salvation. The idea has been projected as an eternal heaven for the Christians and an eternal hell for the non-Christians, particularly for idol-worshipping Hindus. And so far, we do not have major Christian leaders in the world contradicting that statement.

To date, there is no major Christian leader, or Moslem leader, in the world, who is saying that Hinduism is as good as Christianity or Islam. I do not know of any Christian leaders in the West who would say that a Rama or a Krishna is equal to a Jesus. I do not know of any of them who would honor a Ramana Maharshi, a Sri Aurobindo or a Mahatma Gandhi as a God-realized or self-realized sage. I realize there may be some exceptions to this, in the Indian context. But this is not the case with, and it is also not the official policy of the Vatican. It is not the policy of the Pope at all!

I want to read a statement, from "*The Coming of the Third Millennium*", which was issued very recently by the Pope, in relation to the situation in Asia:

"The Asia Synod will deal with the challenge for evangelization posed by the encounter with ancient religions such as Buddhism and Hinduism. While expressing esteem for the elements of truth in these religions, the Church must make it clear that <u>Christ is the one mediator between God and man and the sole Redeemer of humanity.</u>"

This is a direct quote. Now, what is it saying about religious tolerance? Christ is the only way. The Pope is saying that we accept what is true in these religions, but we do not accept them if they do not follow Jesus as the only way. We still have to convert them. That is the message. This is not a message of tolerance and live and let live. It is not a message of let Hindus have their way and we have ours and both are good. It is not a statement that Buddha or Krishna is equal to Jesus.

It is a statement of exclusivism and my contention is that such exclusivism must breed intolerance. If I think that mine is the only way, how can I be really tolerant and accepting of you, if you follow another way? And such intolerance is going to end up causing conflict, division, disharmony and poor communication. It is going to divide communities and cause problems. So, please bear in mind that, in the Indian context, as Hindus, you have to deal with these religions as the majority of the people in the world are practicing and believing in them, and this conversion process is continuing.

I also think that we should have a free, open, friendly dialogue and discussion on all religious matters, both in terms of social interaction and relative to doctrinal matters. There should be complete freedom of discussion, freedom of criticism and freedom of debate just as we have in science.

What generally happens in the field of conversion is that certain groups are targeted for conversion activity. I would like to discriminate between two different things. One is the change of religion, which people may opt for, based upon open and friendly discussion, debate, dialogue and studies. Nothing is wrong with that. But I would discriminate that from what I would call the "global missionary business".

The global missionary business is one of the largest, perhaps even the largest business in the world. Not only the Catholic Church, but also various Protestant organizations have set aside billions of dollars to convert non-Christians to Christianity. They have trained thousands of workers, have formed various plans of evangelization and conversion and have targeted certain communities for that particular purpose.

This multi-national conversion business is like any multi-national economic business. It is not something that is simply fair and open. It is not simply a dialogue or a discussion.

So what we see with this missionary business is a definite strategy for one religion to convert the members of other religions. This conversion business is not about religious freedom. It is about one religion triumphing over all the other religions. It is about making all the members of humanity follow one religion, giving up and, generally, denigrating the religion they had previously been following.

Why is this conversion business so big in India? Because India is the largest non-Christian country in the world where missionaries have the freedom to act and to propagate. Islamic countries – Pakistan, Bangladesh – do not allow this missionary activity at all. In Saudi Arabia, you cannot even bring a Bible or a picture of Jesus into the country. China, also, does not allow such wide-scale missionary conversion activities.

So India, because of its very openness to and tolerance of these missionaries, has become the target. You know from recent newspapers that one missionary was killed in India, which is unfortunate. But in that same week, fifty Christians were massacred in Indonesia by the Moslems there. The religious violence is going on all over the world and Christians are not always the victims.

In India, for centuries, Hindus have been routinely killed for their religion. Even recently in Kashmir, a number of Hindus were massacred, but you will notice that, in the Western media, the death of Hindus for their religion will never count and will never constitute a story. However, if one missionary – one white man – is killed in India, then these Western countries will retaliate with sanctions, criticise, and take some moral high ground.

Missionary activity has a bloody history of genocide on every continent of the world. I am not going to go into all the details here. The Inquisition was in operation in Goa in India. The British used their influence, though less overtly, to force conversions, and certainly the missionaries had an advantage under colonial rule all over the world. In a number of countries, colonial interests used force and persuasion to bring about conversion.

We are told today that we should forget all about that, even though it has only been a generation or two since the colonial era. I say that we cannot forget so easily because the very religious groups that performed these atrocious acts have not yet apologized. If they recognize that this missionary aggression and violence that was done before 1947; that was done in the 19th century; that was done in Goa; that was done in the Americas was wrong, then why don't we get an apology for it?

You will notice that the Christians in America have made some apologies for what they did to the Native Americans. We have yet to see any apology relative to Hindus. If the missionaries want us to believe that they have changed their ways and are now purely non-violent and charitable, then why do they not at least apologize for what they did in the past?

And why should there be conversions at all? What is the motivation behind most seeking of conversions that is coming out of the Christian background? It is their belief that Christianity is the only true religion, Christ is the only saviour of humanity, Christians gain salvation or heaven and non-Christians gain damnation or hell. That is not a policy of harmony and tolerance but a blueprint for disharmony and conflict.

What ultimately happens when someone who has that attitude comes into a community and converts people? People are taught to reject their ancestors and their traditions. Families are broken up. Division and conflict almost inevitably occur wherever this missionary business goes on.

There are actually many forms of Christianity and several different kinds of Christian missionary activity going on. And there are Christian groups in India that are not missionary at all, for example, the old Greek Orthodox and the Syrian Christians, but which represent old and tolerant traditions. Then there is the Catholic tradition which is promoting its missionary activity all over the world but which is doing it in a more subtle way today. They are no longer using the force that they once used in the colonial era, but they are still aiming at global conversion. There are also the old Protestants, the Anglicans and the Lutherans, who are still promoting various types of missionary activity. That has gotten reduced to some degree as well.

However, there is a new Evangelical force in the world today, particularly that coming out of the United States. What are the fundamentalist Christian groups of America? The World Vision, the Christian Coalition, groups like Jehovah's Witnesses, Mormons, Baptists and so on.

They are very actively asking for donations in America in order to convert Hindus in India. We see this routinely in the various television channels that they have. Pat Robertson, one of their main leaders, has said that Hinduism is a demonic religion. They show Hindu gods with animal heads and say, "Oh! Look at how primitive these people are." They look at the political and social problems of India and say; "These are all owing to Hinduism. Please donate money to our cause so we can go to India and convert these people from this horrible religion that they have."

These same Evangelical missionaries are going all over the world and also targeting Catholics. Recently, in Brazil, the Pope called these Evangelical missionaries "wolves" because of what they were doing to, what he termed, "his flock of Christians", which was converting them to their form of Christianity.

So this missionary threat continues and some missionaries are going back to the old hell-fire, damnation, condemnation of Hinduism such as the Catholics used to do in the Middle Ages and in the colonial era. So do not believe that there is religious harmony all over the world and that the other religions respect Hinduism and are willing to live together quietly with Hindus.

In fact, in textbooks in America, it is taught that Hinduism is not a religion because Hinduism does not have only one God, one Book and is not a missionary religion seeking to convert or conquer the world.

So it is this missionary business which needs to be questioned and not simply conversion. And do not be naive about it! There is a consistent use of social upliftment and charity to promote conversion. While social upliftment and charity are very good things, they should be separated from religious conversion. If you want to raise up a country and help them economically, please do so, but do not bring religion into it. When you put the picture of Jesus everywhere obviously religion and conversion are part of your motivation.

You will note that no country in the world has been raised up economically by religious conversion. What has made Japan a great country economically and what made the United States a great country economically are economic means, not a change of religion. Christian countries include some of the poorest countries in the world. The Philippines is the most Catholic and the oldest Christian country in Asia. It remains one of the poorest countries in Asia and has one of the greatest gaps between the rich and the poor.

The most devout Catholics in the world are in Central and South America. They are certainly not found in North America and in Europe, where Christians are more nominal than strong believers. Central and South America also have tremendous social inequality and a tremendous gap between the rich and the poor. But the Catholics there are not telling the poor people that they should convert to another religion in order to raise themselves economically.

So this whole attack on Hindu society by stating that we will raise the poor on religious grounds is based upon the motivation of conversion. Then there is the whole issue of hospitals, orphanages and schools. It is all very wonderful to selflessly help other people. But why do you have to put a religious form there? As long as the picture of Jesus is there, particularly when you have a two thousand year history of aggressive conversion activities, how can you expect people to believe that there is no seeking of conversion? That it is purely selfless service and love of God?

If we love God, if we love our fellow human beings, we will love them regardless of what their religious belief is. We will love their religion as well. We will honor and respect their religion whether they are aboriginal people, Hindus, Buddhists, Zoroastrians, Moslems or Christians. We will not see any need to convert them. In fact, we should not even be conscious of their religion at all. True love of God does not seek converts. It is not based upon names, forms or identity. It is based upon recognizing the Divine presence in all.

One of the great swamis of India, Swami Rama Tirtha, when he came to America, was asked about religion. He said, "You do not belong to any religion. All religions belong to you."

The human being is not a property of any church. You are not something which is owned by anyone or anything. The soul does not need to be saved. It is the eternal and immortal part of our nature. We need only understand the Divine within us. You cannot change the nature of any human being. Hinduism is based upon respecting each individual and the *svadharma* of each individual. We should have many paths and many religions. The idea of only one religious faith for all humanity is like having only one set of clothing for all humanity. It is like people having to eat only one type of food, or people having only one type of job. There should be diversity, abundance and freedom in the religious realm as well.

Unfortunately, all religions do not have the same goal. Religions have various goals. Religions are various paths. We should note that all religions are not theistic. There are non-theistic religions like Buddhism and Jainism where there is no creator God. There are religions with a multiplicity of deities. Monotheism is not the only form of religion in the world and it is not the best form either. All forms of religious worship have their validity and Hinduism recognizes them whether they are polytheism, monotheism or monism. Even atheists have their place in Hinduism. People should have complete freedom to reject religion if that is what they want to do.

Hindu tradition is a *sādhanā* tradition that aims at spiritual practice for self-realization. Most Christian traditions, for example the Protestant tradition, claim that faith alone is enough to save you. This means that a person may be a mass murderer, but if on his deathbed he converts to Christianity, he will go to heaven. Another person may live the life of a saint, but if he does not convert to Christianity, there will be no heaven for him.

Recently, in the United States, a woman who had been convicted of murder was converted to Christianity on death-row and the Christian leaders – particularly the fundamentalist Christians – asked for the death sentence to be removed because since that woman had converted to Christianity therefore the sin no longer counted. The same people would not have made the statement had the woman converted to Hinduism or any other non-Christian faith.

We do need religious harmony and dialogue throughout the world. One of the most unfortunate things is that there is so much misinformation and even disinformation about Hinduism in the world. For example, in the *New York Times*, only last year, there was a story about the Amarnath pilgrimage in India. And what did the *New York Times* call it? "Hindus going to worship the sex organs of Shiva, the God of Destruction." What kind of tolerance is that? What kind of point of view is being projected by it?

But I have to tell you that the fault for this is not really all with these Western people. The fault lies with Hindus themselves. They have been very poor at expressing what their religion is and in countering disinformation and propaganda against them. They do not study their religion properly and so, they cannot explain what it is. They are also misinformed about other religions and think that other religions are just Hinduism in another form. But you will not find these rich traditions of yoga, meditation, Vedas and Vedanta, in other traditions. Particularly in the Protestant tradition in the West, they are rejected almost altogether and, to these Evangelical Christians, they are considered to be the work of the devil.

Some people say that all religions teach the same thing. Well, Hinduism teaches the Law of Karma and Rebirth. Christianity and Islam do not accept that. Some people say all religions teach the same things and they only differ in inessentials. Is the Law of Karma and the process of Rebirth something inessential?

Now, certainly there should be a respect for universal, ethical values such as truthfulness, non-violence, peace and harmony. These should be accepted for all human beings regardless of their religion. In fact, they should be projected for all of nature. One of the problems that I see in Christianity, as most Christians believe it, is that animals are considered to be devoid of a soul and only human beings can gain salvation.

One of the reasons that we are exploiting and destroying this planet is because we do not see the presence of a soul and consciousness in nature, the animals and the rest of the Universe. We must move beyond all our narrow, human-centric creeds. True religion is not a matter of name, form or identity. It is a matter of that which is eternal, that which is universal, that which no one owns and is a matter of consciousness, awareness and Truth.

The highest goal of the Hindu religion is self-realisation, not simply knowing God, but understanding who we are and the Divine presence within us. One of the main problems of humanity is that we do not understand ourselves and our motivations. Instead, based upon some dogma or belief, we are trying to get others to think and act like we do before we understand ourselves and understand them.

So let there be a dialogue. Let there be open, friendly and also critical communication in religion just as in science. But please let us expose and put an end to this missionary business and let us not think that the missionary business is tolerant. The missionary business is not about freedom of religion. It is about the triumph of one religion. It is not about secularism. The missionary business accepts that only one religion is true. It is a religious war aimed at religious control.

The way to challenge this is not through violence or through intolerance, but through being properly informed. It is through being open, friendly, dialoguing and talking to people, so they understand what the Hindu point of view is, so that any distortions about Hinduism are removed. We are all the same Divine being. We all share the same human nature and we must recognise that in all human beings for harmony to exist.

At the same time, we should not be naive about the forces of the world and the forces that are trying to disintegrate this society and this culture. I think it would be a tremendous loss if India gave up Hinduism and became another Christian or Islamic country. We have enough of these already. India has a wealth of its own spiritual traditions that the rest of the world needs.

Why do Westerners come here? They come here for this wealth of spiritual knowledge. In fact, you should be exporting your religion. That is one thing you have enough of. There are other more important things that you need to import.

# 12

# The Debate Goes On

As a follow-up to my debate with Archbishop Arulappa, Pope John Paul II visited India in November 1999, about the time that I was finishing this book. Ashok Singhal, head of VHP, and other Hindu leaders asked the Pope to declare that "all religions were equal and that Christianity was not the only path to salvation." The VHP also asked him to apologize for Christian conversion efforts done by force or intimidation.

The Pope's spokesman in India, Archbishop Alan de Lastic, president of the United Christian Forum for Human Rights, refused on both counts, citing that it was a matter of freedom of religion that allowed for conversion. He made no statement that other religions like Hinduism were valid, nor did he question the conversion process as did Archbishop Arulappa. There was no recognition of past wrongs nor any courtesy at all for genuine Hindu concerns given Christianity's past and its ongoing doctrines of exclusivity. Clearly this Christian Forum for Human Rights is really a forum to promote Christianity.

Typical of the pro-Christian media bias Singhal was called a "Hindu hardliner" for questioning the Pope, though Singhal made a statement affirming religious pluralism, which involved accepting religions other than Hinduism as valid. The Pope, meanwhile, was not criticized, though his refusal to accept other religions as equal to Christianity is clearly intolerant.

About the same time the United States government released a paper on religious freedom in the world, prepared by Robert A. Seiple, the American Ambassador-at-large for

International Religious Freedom. Seiple is not a seasoned diplomat, sensitive to other cultures and religions as would be expected for the post. He was for eleven years the head of World Vision, the largest privately funded relief and development organization in the world, which is a Christian charity and connected to various missionary activities.

Seiple was a former President of Eastern Baptist Theological Seminary. He is a Christian missionary, which on the Protestant side is dominated by the Baptists. A person with such a background is obviously inappropriate for the role that he was given, which would be like giving it to a Catholic priest. It reflects an American religious bias not a diplomatic sensitivity and objectivity. Not surprisingly, his report on religious freedom highlights oppression of Christians but ignores oppression perpetrated by Christians, as if Christian groups were entirely innocent of wrong doing anywhere!

Such major Christian organizations are only interested in a religious freedom that allows them to denigrate other beliefs and convert people. They are unwilling to recognize, much less apologize for the bloody history of missionary activity. And if you question them, they will try to turn you into the one who is intolerant about religion, even if you accept the validity of many paths!

Meanwhile the Southern Baptists in America declared that Hinduism is a religion of darkness ruled by the Devil and sent out thousands of prayer books to this affect. The Southern Baptists are no mere radical fringe group but the largest Protestant sect in America with over fifteen million members. They include both President Clinton and Vice-President Gore among their members and Ambassador Seiple as well, none of whom has specifically criticized them for their views. They asked all Christians to pray to remove the darkness of Hinduism and its many idols and replace it with the light of Christ.

Such groups make the same charges against New Age

Americans who explore occult and spiritual traditions outside of orthodox Christianity. They are also still trying to stop the theory of evolution from being taught in American schools and have made headway in several midwestern States! So much for the idea that American Christians are modern and secular. America includes some of the most backward religious groups in the world.

While in the modern world it is no longer acceptable to use racial slurs because these promote conflict and hatred, religious slurs, particularly against Hindus, are still in vogue, though they are products of the same intolerance and bring about the same misunderstandings. While it is considered to be wrong to call a black person in America a nigger, one can still call Hindus idolaters and devil-worshippers. Which, I ask you, is worse and causes more intolerance, to ridicule a person's race or to demonize his culture and religion? This denigration of non-White religious traditions also reflects racist attitudes.

About this time I was asked to do an interview for Rediff, one of the largest India sites on the Internet, on the Pope's Visit to India, the full text of which is below. VHP of India has also turned the interview into a booklet.

**Rediff Interview**

1. *Could you explain your stance on Pope John Paul II's visit? Since there is a convergence many a times on his role as the religious head of the Catholic Church and the symbolic leader of the Vatican, in your view, in what capacity does he really come to India?*

China, Taiwan and Sri Lanka refused the Pope's request to visit and launch his new activities that aim at the evangelization of Asia. Hindu majority India, though not a Christian country, has allowed him to do so. Therefore the Pope should feel grateful to the tolerant people of India. Clearly no Western country would give a state welcome to a

Hindu religious leader seeking to promote Hindu conversion activities in the West.

India is one of the few countries that recognize the pope as a head of state. The United States and most Western countries recognize the pope only as a religious leader. Clearly the Pope is not coming to India as the political leader of a secular state but as a religious leader. He is conducting a religious mass in Delhi, not organizing a trade mission.

The Catholic Church has a long and self-proclaimed policy of evangelization or conversion and a special Asia Synod to convert Asia. The Pope is coming to India to promote the cause of Catholicism, which means the conversion of Hindus. Naturally he will be friendly in this capacity, but his purpose has an obvious ulterior motive. He is not coming here because he wants to make a pilgrimage to honor the great yogis and swamis of India or to visit her great temples and *tīrthas*.

Today the Catholic Church is losing power in the West. Most Catholics are only nominal in their beliefs. For example, most American Catholics practice birth control that the Church does not approve of and don't attend church on a regular basis. The average age of priests and nuns is nearing the age of sixty and few younger people are coming in. The Church can still get a fair amount of money from rich Western economies but is clearly an institution in decline. Without replenishing its population base it is facing a severe crisis. India offers perhaps the best possibility for doing this with a large population with a history of religious devotion and monastic activity that could readily become priests and nuns.

*2. Why do you believe it is important for him to apologise to the Hindus for the forced conversions in India?*

The bloody history of the Church in America, Africa and Asia is an open book and well known. The Native Americans where I live in the United States still tell stories about how the feet of their people were cut off for refusing to walk to Church or their tongues cut off for refusing to recite prayers.

The Church has claimed that its intolerance is a thing of the past. Yet even if one accepts that it has stopped today, which is debatable, it certainly went on well into this century. That the Church was prominent in Nazi Germany and the Fascist Italy, and never really opposed Hitler or Mussolini, should not be forgotten.

The point is that if you don't apologize how can other groups believe that you have really given up the attitudes that caused such behavior? Such conversion efforts are hurtful to the communities they target, even if no overt violence is involved. The Church has harmed many Hindu families and communities and is still willing to do so, by turning people against their native beliefs and customs.

Christians have made some apologies to the Native Americans and the black Africans for their oppression of them. Why don't Hindus count in this? Aren't they also human beings?

*3. There have been many deeds in history and at present that have gone by without apologies and accountability. Is it worthwhile to resurrect such issues in the present context? What purpose does this serve?*

The problem is that the same attitudes and behavior that resulted in such violence in the past still go on today. The official policy of the Catholic Church today is still that Hinduism, Buddhism, Jainism, Sikhism and other Indian religions are not valid or true. This promotes division, misunderstanding and can still lead to violence.

Today we have given up the doctrine of racial superiority that the White Europeans used to justify their colonial rule. But the attitude of religious superiority – that only Christianity is true and the other religions are false – still goes on. Such religious exclusivism like racism is backward and prejudicial. If I believe, as the Church teaches, that my non-Catholic neighbors will go to hell, it doesn't do much for communal harmony. And new converts take these beliefs much more seriously.

*4. What are the atrocities perpetrated against Hindus by the Christians that you would like to see the Pope apologise about? Can you name some of these crimes?*

The Goa Inquisition was probably the worst and involved torture and murder of thousands of Hindus and the destruction of many Hindu temples over a period of several decades. It was done by the same groups that promoted the genocide of Native Americans. But Church policy all along has been that Hinduism is bad and unless Hindus convert they cannot be saved. This easily gives rise to excesses. After all if I believe that if you don't join my religion you will suffer in eternal hell, for your benefit I must do everything possible, which easily leads to excesses.

*5. What are the reasons for the sudden anger against the Christians?*

The anger is not so much sudden as that today we have a more aware Hindu populace and a larger media forum for airing such grievances. Oppressed religious and social groups of all types are now making such protests. Christians will more quickly protest against Hindus if they feel that Hindus are not treating them fairly. Hindus have actually protested a lot less than other groups, though they have more commonly been the targets of denigration. Such a Hindu awakening was inevitable. The real question is why it took so long.

Another issue is that the Hindu reconversion movement has started, which Christians find threatening and highlights this issue.

*6. Why have they replaced Muslims as the hate objects for Hindus? Is it true that the VHP's campaign is driven because Sonia Gandhi is a Christian?*

I don't think that Hindus hate Christians. They are not targeting Christians for conversion or calling them devil worshippers as the Southern Baptists, the largest Protestant sect in America to which both Bill Clinton and Al Gore belong, are calling Hindus. Rather Hindus are challenging Christian prejudices against Hindus that cause mistrust and hatred of Hindus by Christians. You will find a picture of Christ in many Hindu homes, but you won't find any picture of Krishna in any Christian homes.

Nor do Hindus hate Muslims. It is the general Muslim view that Hindus are idolaters, polytheists and *kāfirs* and doomed in the eyes of Allah. Hindus have no such doctrines about Islam. Hindu dislike of Christianity and Islam is largely a backlash against the centuries long efforts to convert them which are still going on.

I don't think the VHP campaign would stop if Sonia Gandhi left politics either. That Sonia Gandhi is a Christian may be a matter of concern for Hindus because of the Christian seeking to convert Hindus. Clearly most Christians in America would not be happy if a Hindu became the head of a major American political party, particularly if Hindus were active trying to convert Christians in America.

The greater issue is caused by the increasing Christian evangelization activities in India. Look throughout the country, particularly in the South and you will find them expanding almost everywhere.

Why should there be an evangelization of Asia at all? Don't we live in a global society in which we must recognize pluralism in religion just as we do in culture or language? Are not the great religions of Asia good enough and a great legacy for the entire world? Why do Westerners come to India? It is mainly to find spiritual teachings that they didn't find in their own Western Christian backgrounds.

Others argue that since only about three percent of India has become Christian why should one care? But the areas that have become Christian, like the North-East, are getting progressively alienated from the rest of India and seeking to secede from the country. And the possibility of dramatically more conversions in the future cannot be ruled out. That someone has fired a gun against you and missed is no reason not to take it seriously, particularly if he is loading a better gun for further shots. The point is that it is unkind to begin with.

*7. As a former Catholic why are you suspicious of the Pope's campaign? What is it about Pope John Paul II that makes you suspicious of him?*

As a former Catholic, I am well aware that most Catholics have no real respect for Hinduism. My uncle became a missionary to convert Native Americans and save them from hell, and Hindus are placed in the same category. The current pope is a well-known conservative promoting evangelical activity throughout the world, but he covers his actions with a veneer of social liberalism.

Today no major Catholic leaders in the West are saying that Hinduism is a great and spiritual religion that is worthy of respect like Christianity. Should they succeed in converting Hindu India to Catholicism they would happily put an end to the great Yogic and Vedantic traditions that are perhaps the soul of this country, which would be a great loss to humanity. We have enough Christian countries in the world today, but there is only one India and it is not Christianity which has made the civilization of India unique and great.

Catholicism has a long history of coopting other beliefs. It is willing to give an apparent honor and regard to something, as long as it is placed under the supremacy of Christianity. For example, the Church subordinated the old Pagan Greek philosophies of Aristotle and Plato, which it made the basis of Christian theology. It hopes to do the same thing with Hindu and Buddhist philosophies, which it hopes to fashion as a prelude to the message of Christ.

In South India Catholic priests dress up like Hindu swamis and call their organizations ashrams but are still actively engaged in conversion. Their Hindu dress is not done to honor Hindu traditions but to make Christianity more acceptable to the local population, like McDonalds offering vegetarian burgers in India for Hindus who won't eat the usual hamburger.

Similarly the Pope will probably speak of the greatness of India and the need for brotherhood and human rights but he will certainly not say that Hindus don't need to convert to Christianity. He will portray Christianity as a religion of compassion, equality and democracy to appeal to the poor in India, though historically Christianity has commonly been aligned with monarchies, colonial armies, fascist states and ruling juntas.

Hindus may confuse such statements of general human regard with real religious tolerance or even with an acceptance of Hinduism. They may confuse a coopting of their religion with a real regard for it. The new Catholic strategy is that Hinduism is all right as far as it goes but will only reach its real fulfillment when it accepts Christ. This is the same old conversion ploy, only done in a more covert way. The American Protestants, who still portray Hinduism as a religion of the Devil, are at least more honest about their views and their intentions.

*8. The Pope is a state guest, invited by the Government of India, doesn't the stance of the VHP undermine India's secular tradition and embarrass A B Vajpayee – even his alliance partners do not agree with such protests.*

Not at all. In America visits of foreign heads of states are often marked by protests. When the Chinese president was here recently many Americans, mainly of Chinese ancestry, protested the visit, including some that were democrats. Such protests are part of democracy. Islamic groups in America have protested the visit of Israeli leaders as well. The Pope cannot be made immune to such protests. They are part of secular traditions that don't require the people in any country to bow down to a foreign leader, whether he is a religious figure or not.

*9. If in spite of the pressure applied for the apology, if the Pope does not apologise won't it be a loss of face for the VHP and other organisations demanding for the same?*

I don't think anyone expects the current pope to make such an apology, though a future pope might do so. But the case has to be brought out anyway for the sake of truth and for posterity. The fact that it is coming out is beneficial for Hindus. Hindus have long been too quiet about the attacks against them. Hindus tend to bow down to any religious leader as a holy man, even one who does not respect their traditions or honor their gods and sages. It is actually more important that Hindus change than that the pope changes.

The Pope doesn't want to apologize to Hindus because he doesn't want to recognize Hinduism as a valid religion. He won't even mention the word Hinduism. He will call Diwali an Indian cultural festival, not a Hindu religious event.

*10. What impact do you think the Pope's visit is going to have on socio-religious culture of India?*

Hopefully it will make Hindus more savvy about what is going on in the world. Current missionary plans to convert India, both by Catholics and Protestants, are the greatest in history in terms of financial backing, media manipulation and manpower support. An entire new attack is being launched. China is also emerging as a new target. Religious tolerance is not a one way street. We cannot ask Hindus to honor Christianity when Christians, starting with the pope, don't honor Hinduism, however much they may talk of God, humanity or peace.

Why can't the Pope say that Christianity is not the only way and that Hinduism by itself can be enough? That would be an expression of tolerance and open-mindedness. Why are

Hindus who accept the validity of many paths called "hardliners" while a pope who refuses to do so is honored as a holy man? Is not pluralism a sign of tolerance and exclusivism the hallmark of intolerance?

Catholicism today is not a pluralistic tradition honoring different religious and spiritual paths as valid. It is an exclusivist tradition dominated by a leader who will not accept a Buddha, Krishna, Rama or Guru Nanak as a Son of God but only Jesus. What does that say about how he views India and the kinds of plans he intends to promote here? Hopefully the Pope's visit will get people to really think about these matters.

## A Hindu Response
## to the Pope's Call for Evangelization

These events also inspired me to make a statement on the Pope's call for the evangelization (conversion) of Asia, which I have included below.

The Age of Evangelization is over!

It is now the age of science and spirituality and exclusivist religions of all types, which reflect a medieval mentality, should be discarded as out of date. Evangelization is an effort to impose one religion upon humanity and to eliminate other beliefs as invalid or inadequate.

The idea that only one religion is true is on par with narrow views that only one race or one culture is true. Religious exclusivism belongs to the era of racism and colonialism and reflects a similar bigotry and prejudice.

Asian peoples, oppressed by years of racism, colonialism and missionary activity are now awakening to the value of their own cultures and religions. They now know that there is much more genuine spirituality in their own traditions than in those of the West, which is why many Westerners come to India for spiritual guidance.

The coming planetary age does not belong to the conversion-seeking religions of the West, which divide humanity into the believers and the non-believers, but to the spirituality of consciousness such as revealed in Hindu and Buddhist philosophies which unite humanity into one great family.

It is time for Christians to come to India to learn about God, such as the yogis and swamis of the land have realized, and to stop preaching about a God they do not really know or represent.

We Hindus welcome a new era of Self-realization and God-realization for all people beyond the boundaries of church and dogma, honoring all individuals, all cultures and all spiritual aspiration.

God is not the property of a church or of a belief but is the true Self of all beings. Let us honor that Self in all beings regardless of their religious affiliation.

# 13

# Systems of Vedic Knowledge

The Vedas contain keys both to cosmogenesis and to individual transformation. They provide complete systems of both cosmic and self-knowledge which are interrelated. Our true Self is the universal Self and the world of nature is its manifestation. My encounter with the Vedas extended to different branches of Vedic science, particularly Ayurveda and Vedic Astrology. This is not something unique to me but inherent in Vedic knowledge that helps us understand all life both externally and internally.

I started the Vedic Research Center in 1980 to promote a deeper study of the Vedic mantras. This became the American Institute of Vedic Studies in 1988 with additional programs in Ayurvedic medicine and in Vedic Astrology. But the Vedic mantras remained the foundation, support and goal of all these other disciplines.

## Ayurveda

In India I visited Ayurvedic schools, Ayurvedic companies and Ayurvedic teachers throughout the country. This occurred mainly through the help of Dr. Vashta, who had many connections in this regard. I saw modern trained Ayurvedic doctors who understood allopathic medicine as thoroughly as any Western doctor. But there were also traditionally trained doctors carrying on old family secrets passed on by personal instruction only who shunned modern medicine altogether. Some Ayurvedic doctors used alchemy, healing sounds, and meditation, adding a great spiritual depth to their approach. Others had a profound knowledge of how

170 / <small>HOW I BECAME A HINDU</small>

the body works on an energetic level and how to change it with the right food, diet, exercise and impressions. In addition India, with its biodiversity and wonderful climate, contains a wealth of botanical resources that can be of great help for healing and should not be lost.

I came to understand how this ancient system of healing survived the onslaughts of time and is reviving itself in the modern world. Clearly Ayurveda has a wealth of wisdom to offer all people. It helps us understand our individual constitution and the unique environmental circumstances in which we live. Unfortunately, Ayurveda in India does not have the respect or support due it or necessary to sustain its proper facilities and practices. Like other Vedic teachings it is looked upon as out of date rather than as a form of eternal knowledge.

I began to write a series of books on Ayurveda and also introduced courses in it. With several colleagues we helped found Ayurvedic schools in the West and developed educational material for them. I watched Ayurveda grow rapidly from an obscure foreign healing system to a common part of alternative medicine in the West. I was also surprised to see how readily Ayurveda led people to other aspects of Hindu and Vedic Dharma, perhaps even more so than the study of Yoga did.

Many Western Ayurvedic students are connecting with Hindu deities like Ganesha and Hanuman or Shiva and Durga. They are using mantras and pujas as part of their practices and for the preparation of medicines. They accept the wisdom and healing power of the Vedas and honor the Rishis. Through Ayurveda a Vedic and yogic life-style is gradually being introduced to the West. Vedic concepts like Agni and Vayu are gaining recognition for insight into health both physical and mental as well as for understanding yogic practices. Such a practical Vedic basis will eventually draw people to all aspects of Vedic science.

## Vedic Astrology

I continued to study Vedic Astrology and over time began consultations and teaching of the subject. Just as with Ayurveda I introduced books and courses on it. In 1992 along with several colleagues, we organized the first major Vedic Astrology symposium in America, which was a great success. Dr. B.V. Raman, India's foremost astrologer of the century, was our keynote speaker.

In 1993 we started the American Council of Vedic Astrology (ACVA) which has since become a large organization and has started tutorial and training programs in the subject. Most notably ACVA has succeeded in creating a genuine Vedic Astrology community in the West.

Along with Vedic Astrology I became aware of Vāstu, the Vedic science of sacred geometry, architecture and directional influences. While astrology shows us how to orient ourselves in time, Vāstu shows how to orient ourselves in space. These two aspects of Vedic science are bound to become much more important for the future.

Jyotish (Astrology) provides for *graha-shānti* or harmonizing with celestial forces, the powers of time. Vāstu provides *griha-shānti* or peace in the house or dwelling, the forces of space. These two give us the right orientation in time and space. Ayurveda provides *deha-śuddhi* or purification of the body. Yoga provides *chitta-śuddhi* or purification of the mind. These two give us harmony in our personal life of body and mind. Vedanta provides Self-realization that is the ultimate goal of all these.

Just as with Ayurveda, Western Vedic Astrology students are also interested in mantras, deities and pujas that are an important part of the system, particularly for remedial measures (for balancing planetary influences). Ganesha has become the visible deity of Vedic Astrology in the West. Students are also interested in the planetary deities and the mythology of Vedic Astrology. They see the great wisdom in this subtle science and recognize its Hindu foundations.

## Dr. B.V. Raman

Dr. B.V. Raman was another important figure guiding me on the Vedic path. He is best known as modern India's greatest astrologer. For sixty years up to his death in 1998 he was the leader of the Vedic Astrology movement in India, through his popular *Astrological Magazine* and his many in-depth books on the subject. Most notably, Dr. Raman presented Vedic Astrology in an English idiom that made it accessible both to the English educated elite of India and to foreign audiences. I came across his books in the early seventies but would only come to meet him in India many years later. I eventually took a special initiation with him for the purposes of learning Astrology.

Dr. Raman has given a well-documented set of political predictions over the years, like the rise and fall of Hitler, or the resignation of Richard Nixon, forecasting these events well in advance of their actual occurrence. No other astrologer of the century, East or West, has equaled his record. Yet Dr. Raman was far more than an astrologer. He was a statesman and a thinker, a modern sage with a cosmic vision based upon a deep Vedic perspective. He was a great defender of Vedic values and causes, challenging modern distortions, Eurocentric biases and scientific dogma with clarity, consistency and determination.

Dr. Raman encouraged me not only to develop Vedic Astrology in the West but also to develop the other aspects of my Vedic work. Above all, we shared the same desire to rewrite the history of India in harmony with the vision of the sages. I spoke several times at events in Bangalore that he organized and visited with him on a number of occasions. Dr. Raman looked at my astrological chart according to his special system and provided various insights to help with my life and work that have proved to be invaluable. Vedic

Astrology is a science of karma and can enable us to understand the purpose of our incarnation.

I met with many other astrologers in India, particularly in Delhi, which has a number of good astrologers like Dr. K.S. Charak or Dr. Dinesh Sharma. Most of them are dedicated spiritual Hindus as well and use Hindu mantras and rituals to balance planetary influences. Clearly Vedic Astrology is well and alive. Recently many excellent new books on Vedic Astrology have come out, showing how to use the system in the modern world with breathtaking accuracy and depth!

## Vedic Physics

Vedic science is the science of consciousness. It can integrate spiritual sciences like Yoga with material sciences like Physics. I also had occasion to meet with important scientists introducing a Vedic perspective into the scientific community. Unfortunately, since I am not trained in Physics I haven't always been able to understand what they say.

But clearly all the things that we hear of in modern science like space travel, time travel, entering other dimensions or communicating with beings from other worlds, are already at least imagined in various Hindu texts from the Puranas to the *Yoga-Vāsishtha*. Indeed there is nothing in science or science fiction that the Hindu mind has not already thought about. The main difference is that Hindu Yogis controlled the forces of nature through the power of their own minds and not through technology, which is a much more dangerous way to harness these forces.

It is time for the spiritual science of the Rishis and Yogis to be united with the material science of scientists today. We will undoubtedly see many more great Hindu scientists in the future. And scientists of all backgrounds will be drawn to a Vedantic view of the Universe as Brahman and Atman.

## Sanskrit, the Language of the Gods

The Sanskrit language is a living being. It is Sarasvati or

Vāk, the embodied Goddess of wisdom. The very language itself teaches you, particularly the Vedic language in which sound and meaning closely correspond and the words reflect the cosmic creative force. This is why *Nirukta* or etymology is a limb of the Vedas. It was not just a grammatical study but a means of understanding how the universe is created. Sanskrit is a language of such beauty and brilliance that it captivates the mind and, like a muse, inspires us to deeper insight.

Sanskrit is the vehicle for what Hinduism really is. To discover the essence of Hinduism one should learn Sanskrit and contact its power, beauty and depth. Most of the prejudices against Hinduism disappear when one learns the language behind it and the actual meaning of its terms and principles which are so easily distorted in their English renderings. Language is the basis of culture. The language of a country carries its entire cultural legacy. Through Sanskrit one can come into contact with the wisdom of India and its many sages who transcended our ordinary human awareness and contacted realms far beyond both body and mind.

Yet Sanskrit is more than just a language of India, it is the very language of the Gods and the spiritual language of humanity. Until we as a species discover Sanskrit, the native language of the soul, our culture is bound to be confused and will lack connection with our higher spiritual purpose. Sanskrit also helps us understand science, as it is a language that reflects cosmic intelligence and its unfoldment.

I have done much *mantra-sādhanā* with special *bīja-mantras* that I have received. This has probably been my most important spiritual practice. Such mantras change the energetics of the mind and make it receptive to higher forces. They connect us with the deities or powers of consciousness that govern the universe. The original Vedic Yoga is based on mantra, not *āsana* or yoga postures. Mantras are like *āsanas* for the mind and make it flexible to become a vehicle for the higher Self (Paramātmā).

In 1996 I visited Askharam, the headquarters of Samskrita

Bharati and was interviewed for their magazine *Sambhāshuna Sandeśa*. Samskrita Bharati is the main Sanskrit organization in India. It has done crucial work teaching conversational Sanskrit to millions of people and reviving Sanskrit as a living language throughout the country.

Krishna Shastri, head of the Samskrita Bharati movement later visited with me in the United States. He was a young man and a dynamic speaker and charismatic personality. He could get anyone to start speaking Sanskrit, even those who knew nothing of the script or the grammar. The living power of Sanskrit comes through him. This new Sanskrit movement is essential for the revival of Hinduism.

Hinduism has its own language, which is perhaps the greatest of all human languages and the very language of creation. Sanskrit provides a firm foundation on which all of Vedic and Yogic science, on which all of human knowledge, can be built and integrated according to a higher purpose.

### *Yajñas*, Pujas and Temples

Vedic *Yajñas* or sacrifices were not mere primitive rituals but sophisticated and scientific ways of harnessing the secret powers of nature to affect changes in our karma, both individually and collectively. These *yajñas* center on fire rituals and fire offerings. Fire is the elemental force through which we can connect with all the powers of nature. As the central of the five elements it mediates between the formless spiritual realms above (air and ether) and the formed material realms below (earth and water).

Hindu devotional rituals or pujas are precise practices to connect us with the higher worlds of intelligence, joy and creativity that oversee this lower, limited physical realm. Pujas generate subtle influences (*tanmātras*) that link us with the deities or cosmic powers. Our real role as human beings includes performing such rituals to link this physical world with the subtle realms beyond, without which we remain isolated in the darkness of the senses.

Hindu temples are scientifically designed instruments to

gather and magnify our higher aspirations on a collective level. They serve to link the human world with the Divine world. The temple icons channel higher energies and deeper knowledge to us. They allow astral forces to become embodied in the physical world. They allow the Gods to descend and work among us. The great temples of South India are probably the best example of this. I keep many *mūrtis* (Hindu icons) in my home, which is a kind of temple. I have Shiva, Devi in many forms, Ganesha, Hanuman, Vishnu, Rama, and more. They serve as a constant reminder that we are not alone but live in a universe permeated with Divine forces. I see no contradiction between such images and the formless Absolute (Brahman). They represent the many sides of Brahman which is infinite.

## Vedic Ecology

The Vedic worldview is firmly rooted in honoring our Mother Earth, for which various forms of Earth worship or Bhumi-Puja are prescribed. For proper meditation we must first do prayers to sanctify the ground on which we sit. Vedic Ecology reflects this Vedic methodology for connecting with the Earth and helping unfold her many secret powers. Vedic rituals and Hindu Pujas are part of this process.

The Earth is not inanimate but a force of hidden consciousness unfolding a secret Divine Will for the higher evolution of all creatures. The Earth is the Divine Mother incarnate. In the wilderness she is Pārvati, the wife of Shiva, who leads us to wisdom and transcendence. In the fertile plains she is Lakshmi, the wife of Vishnu, who bestows love and nurturance.

Unfortunately, most Hindus have forgotten this Vedic view of the Earth and don't protect their natural environment. They have not added a Hindu point of view to the ecology movement, which is perhaps the main idealistic movement in the world today. Hinduism can help spiritualize the ecology movement and reconnect it with our ancient sense of the sacred Earth Mother and give us the tools to communicate with her. But this requires awakened Hindus who understand this tradition and its importance.

Part of the challenge of modern Hinduism is to reclaim its connection to the Earth. Bharat Mata or Mother India is also Bhumi Mata or Mother Earth. India embodies the Earth and its perennial wisdom by its connection with the Sun. Healing the Earth should be integral to all Hindu causes and to all spirituality everywhere.

## Yoga

Yoga in the broader sense refers to the different spiritual paths of *jñāna* (knowledge), *bhakti* (devotion), *karma* (service) and *rāja-yoga* (internal practices). Yoga is the essence of the Vedic approach that involves uniting us with the greater universe of consciousness. It is the technology that applies Vedic wisdom in an experiential manner. Yoga is the main practice of Hinduism, which from its music and dance to its philosophy and medicine employs yogic methods and insights. Once one understands the Hindu roots of Yoga and the Yogic orientation of Hinduism, one's practice of yoga is enriched and one's understanding of Hinduism becomes authentic.

I visited various Yoga centers and ashrams such as exist throughout in India. Among the most interesting was Vivekananda Yoga Kendra in Bangalore. This broad-based organization teaches Yoga in a comprehensive manner, including spirituality and psychology, and also takes a rigorous scientific perspective. It conducts large conferences bringing important people from all over the world. It shows the integrality of Yoga, Vedanta and Hinduism, which function best when used together. Such schools show how Yoga is developing in India and reaching out to the world. Many more such institutions are necessary for the future. They are more important than churches or temples.

# 14

# Towards a New Western Hinduism

## Western Yoga Teachers and Yoga Groups

In the period from the mid-eighties I worked with various Western yoga groups. While this occurred mainly through Ayurvedic medicine I brought in the Vedas, Vedic Astrology, Vedanta and Hinduism. I tried to present an integral Ayurveda that did not stop with the body but considered *prāṇa*, mind and consciousness – a full life science.

In the process I came to know many leaders in the Yoga field, both Western *āsana* experts and prominent gurus from India. I was able to experience their teachings first hand and learned how they functioned behind the scenes. In the process I discovered that few American yoga students considered themselves to be Hindus. Few knew what Hinduism was. Many blindly accepted common media and missionary stereotypes as true. Most didn't know Vedanta or what the Vedas dealt with. Many didn't regard these as important.

Many were connected to a particular guru from India but had little sense of the tradition behind the teacher. Their tendency was to look to their specific teacher as the source of the teaching, the avatar of a new universal religion, and not a traditional Hindu. Others were so busy popularizing yoga that they didn't take the time to really understand its background. The result was that the American Yoga movement lacked connection with the greater Yoga tradition and its Hindu foundation. It often slipped into commercialism, if not vulgarity.

In America the outward and physical aspects of yoga predominate with a cultural fixation on the body. The sensational aspects of spirituality are also popular, with a seeking of quick spiritual experiences and the tendency to create personality cults. In America everything becomes a business. The result is that the teacher with the best advertising and self-promotion becomes the most famous and is looked upon as the authority, though their real knowledge may be limited.

Yet more and more yoga students do want to know the tradition behind Yoga and are not content merely to be good at yoga postures. Over time I have seen an increase in Hindu elements in the Western yoga community. Hindu deities like Shiva, Devi, Krishna and Ganesha are becoming accepted. Hindu chants, songs and rituals are getting popular. There is a growing interest in Sanskrit. A new interest is arising in Vedanta through teachers like Ramana Maharshi and in Yoga philosophy through the *Yogasūtras*.

Other aspects of Hindu Dharma are coming into the yoga community including Ayurveda, Vedic Astrology, and Vāstu. People are drawing connections between these disciplines and noting their common basis. Once a person has been exposed to this broader culture of Hinduism, they usually go deeper into the system. Hinduism is percolating into the West through various avenues and incarnations. Because of misconceptions about Hinduism, American yoga students may say they are not Hindus. Yet if you explain Sanātana Dharma to them, including karma, rebirth, *sādhanā* and Self-realization they quickly accept such a teaching as the approach that they follow.

**The New Age Movement**

Christian fundamentalists in America see Hinduism as their main threat through the New Age movement, a fact that they have highlighted in various books and programs. They refer to the New Age movement in America as an American

Hinduism taking shape. They identify both the New Age and Hinduism as the same old paganism, idolatry and pursuit of the occult that the *Bible* criticizes. Their recent aggressive missionary effort in India is a counterattack against the Hindu guru influence in America that they have long felt threatened by.

However, the New Age movement in America is a diverse phenomenon. It includes votaries of every sort of mystical tradition East and West, much interest in Native American and shamanic traditions, and a strong fascination with the occult, astral travel, channeling, Atlantis, UFOs and ETs (Extra Terrestrials). It is allied with every form of alternative medicine, bodywork, new psychology and self-actualization movement. It has a strong vegetarian, pacifistic and pro-ecology tendency. There is a new Paganism in it, with a growing interest in ancient Celtic, Greek, Egyptian, Babylonian and Minoan lore. There are Native African elements as well with a similar movement starting among Black Americans.

Yet most New Age people do share a belief in karma and reincarnation. They accept the existence of a Creator but also look to a higher Self. In this regard their underlying philosophy is like Vedanta. Many New Agers look up to India and its gurus, even if they are not disciples.

Though the New Age movement has much fantasy, if not self-indulgence within it, as it matures it will probably come to resemble Hinduism that broadly accepts all means of accessing higher awareness. A new futuristic form of Hinduism or Sanātana Dharma is likely to arise combining a resurgence of the Vedic tradition from India, related mystical, native and Pagan traditions throughout the world, as well as futuristic ideas for the coming planetary age. An awakened and expanded Hinduism may indeed become the planetary religion in form as it has always been in spirit. For this Hindus need to reach out to such groups and forge a common alliance with them.

## American Hinduism

Hinduism never seemed to be something foreign or alien to me or inappropriate to my circumstances living in the West. It is the very religion of nature and consciousness in the broadest sense, which makes it relevant to everyone. For me true religion and spirituality comes from nature. It arises from the ground. The soul in nature lives beneath the earth, in the soil, dwelling in the roots of plants and sustaining the vegetable kingdom. The fire at the center of the Earth that upholds geological processes on the planet is a form of the Divine fire that dwells within our hearts.

The most important insights that have come to me usually occur while walking in nature, particularly hiking in the high mountains. In the wilderness nature can enter into our consciousness and cleanse our minds of human-centered compulsions. I think that liberation is like wandering off into nature, climbing up a high mountain, and not coming back to the lowlands of human society.

Hinduism is a religion of the Earth. It honors the Earth as the Divine Mother and encourages us to honor her and help her develop her creative potentials. The deities of Hinduism permeate the world of nature. For example, Shiva is the God of the mountains, while Pārvati is the mountain Goddess. Shiva dwells in high and steep rocky crags and cliff faces. Pārvati rules over mountain streams, waterfalls, and mountain meadows with their many flowers.

Hiking in the mountain country one can find natural Shiva lingas. Beneath high rocky peaks that take the form of a linga, a basin naturally forms as a mountain lake that becomes the yoni. In this way Shiva and Pārvati manifest everywhere in nature. They don't belong to a single country or book only. It is not necessary to live in India to be a Hindu. In fact one must live in harmony with the land where one is located to be a true Hindu.

I see Hinduism as a religion eminently suited for all lands

and for all people because it requires that we connect with the land and its creatures – that we align our individual self with the soul of all beings around us. Hinduism finds holy places everywhere, wherever there is a river, a mountain, a large rock, or big tree, wherever there is some unusual natural phenomenon be it a spring, a cave, or a geyser.

In this way I can speak of an American Hinduism and call myself an American and a Hindu – an American connected with the land and a Hindu connected with the spirit and soul of that land. Hinduism has helped me discover the forces of nature in which I live, their past and their future, their unique formations and their connections with the greater universe and the cosmic mind.

A real American Hinduism would not be a Hinduism scaled down to the needs of American commercialism, turned into a new fad or hype of Hollywood or Wall Street. It isn't merely yoga postures for football players or for movie stars. It is an experience of one's Self and true nature not only in the context of the American landscape but also as connected with the Earth, universe and the supreme consciousness.

Hinduism honors the Divine Self in all beings and helps us develop our individual potentials organically and in harmony with all of life. That is why it can never accept any final dogma or prescribe any stereotyped creed or practice for everyone. Its goal is to help us realize ourselves through learning about the universe we live in that is a reflection of our deeper soul.

As time continues this Hindu sense of the cosmic Self and world Soul will dawn on more and more people, regardless of their location or culture. It is simply the unfoldment of life itself and its deeper spirit. This will gradually transform humanity and bring us back into the fold of the universal religion beyond names and institutions. We will once more become caring citizens of the conscious universe instead of human-centered exploiters of the natural world as we are today.

# 15

# Conclusion

Hindu Dharma came to me over a long period of time, in many forms, through many people, as well as through a deeper consciousness. From leaving the Catholic Church to officially becoming a Hindu took a number years. It was never a question of leaving one religion and looking for another one better, but of a quest for truth at a spiritual level. This at first made all outer religious formalities irrelevant but later showed me the importance of culture and community in sustaining one's spiritual path.

Disturbed by media or textbook images of Hinduism or bewildered by its multifaceted nature, people ask me: "Can one access the deeper teachings of Hinduism, like Yoga and Vedanta, without having to go through the outer aspects of the religion as caste, ritual or temple worship? Does one need to formally become a Hindu to benefit from its spiritual teachings?"

One must cast off prevalent misconceptions about Hindu Dharma before being able to answer these questions. Hindu Dharma does not dwell in a mere formal social identity, but in following one's own dharma. Its rituals reflect nature and are not artificial. Its deities symbolize different aspects of our higher Self and the cosmic mind. While one doesn't have to officially become a Hindu before being able to use its teachings, one cannot access the deeper aspects of Hinduism without becoming something like a Hindu in one's life and mentality.

One might also ask, What would an American or a Westerner have to lose by becoming a Hindu? You would have to give up exclusive beliefs that say that there is only

one true God, prophet, savior or scripture. You would have
to become reconciled to your Pagan ancestors and respect
their way of life. You would have to accept pluralism in
religion. You would have to bring spirituality into your daily
life through some form of prayer, chanting, study,
contemplation or meditation. But you wouldn't have to stop
thinking, or cease to be open to the truth. You wouldn't need
to restrict yourself to any creed or dogma. Above all, you
wouldn't have to give yourself away in the process. You
would need only to strive to understand yourself at a deeper
and universal level.

## The Importance of Culture

Being a Hindu means recognizing the spiritual teachings
that have most helped me in life. The name is not of great
importance. The tradition behind it is what matters.
Hinduism, Hindu Dharma, Sanātana Dharma, Yoga, Vedanta,
yogic spirituality, Vedic science and other such terms reflect
different aspects of this same vast teaching. Yet we must
settle on one name for convenience of communication in the
modern world and that appears to be Hinduism because this
term has already gained recognition. There is no reason why
the other positive appellations of this tradition cannot be felt
with the term Hindu Dharma, except for the rigidity of
unquestioned anti-Hindu stereotypes in our culture.

Personally I believe that Hinduism, particularly as defined
as Sanātana Dharma, is the best religion in the world.
Hinduism has the most holy books, the most Gods and
Goddesses, the most sages and yogis, the most temples and
tīrthas, and the most intricate knowledge of the occult and
spiritual planes. It is the oldest of religions and the most
diverse and the most adaptable, which are all points of great
merit.

Yet it doesn't bother me if someone else prefers another
religion anymore than if someone else would prefer a
different food. Let there be abundance in the spiritual life, as
in all life. Let people follow whatever religion elevates their

hearts and minds. Let each person have his or her own religion, as each one of us is a Divine Soul with a unique perspective on life. Let each one of us become a God or Goddess in our deeper consciousness, free of all dependency upon external forms and limitations. Away with sin and guilt. Let the Divine arise within everyone!

The ultimate goal of human life is to transcend culture and personality to the unconditioned pure being. But the means to do this is through our culture and way of life. Perhaps this sounds contradictory. The goal is to reach the infinite and eternal. But we must do this from our particular standpoint in time and space, body and mind. Our individuality is embedded in a certain cultural matrix and its forms, just as the language that we learn to speak shapes our thoughts. To reach the universal we must have the right organic foundation at a local level. We need to create a culture that can lead us to it, by helping us discovering our cosmic potentials at an individual level. This is what Hindu Dharma provides in many different ways.

The spiritual life is an eonic journey, taking many lifetimes and leading us through many different worlds. Very few souls, only a handful in each generation, will complete their journey in a particular incarnation. Spiritual growth requires the proper culture and tradition to sustain our collective aspiration from life to life. Otherwise a few rare individuals may be able to progress spiritually but the great majority cannot go far, just as only a few of the many seeds cast on uncultivated ground can flourish.

## The Future of the Planet

Today humanity has created a civilization that is against nature. We have a science and technology that is against life. We have religions that are against spirituality. Unless we counter these trends much difficulty lies ahead for our species and for the planet that we at present rudely dominate. I am not speaking of some impending end of the world or cataclysms such as abound in New Age and Christian fundamentalist thinking. But the next century is facing many potential problems, if not calamities.

There is a real danger of progressively devastating eco-catastrophes, natural disasters like floods, earthquakes and climate changes. Some of these occur in the normal course of history, but today we have too many people and cities in vulnerable areas like flood plains and deserts. Other environmental problems will be created or magnified by our disruption of the forests and the biosphere. Along with this environmental imbalance new diseases may arise, not only physically but also psychologically, as we lose the organic root of life through which alone real health and happiness is possible.

Our food, water and air are poor in quality if not toxic. Most of the impressions that we take in through the mass media are disturbing if not violent. Our genetic quality is declining with mindless reproduction and poor education. We may be developing our outer personalities and advancing technologically but our soul is stifled. While the situation is far from hopeless it does require determined action to avoid major difficulties from arising in the next few decades.

Spiritual teachings like Hindu Dharma show us how to counter these negative trends. They guide us how to live in harmony with nature and with a higher consciousness without having to sacrifice reason or give up the benefits of science. We must, as the ancients did, return to the Sun and create a new technology of solar power. We must create a clean technology that does not damage the environment or pollute the Earth. We must learn to channel not only the outer energy of the Sun but also its healing power and its higher intelligence.

The Vedas are said to be inherent in the rays of the Sun, which hold the life, light and love that manifests on Earth. Let us once more open up to this solar wisdom and connect with our solar Self, our true being of the light of consciousness, compassion and truth. Let us not forget the great *Gāyatrī-mantra* of the *Rigveda*:

*May we meditate upon the supreme effulgence of the Divine solar creator, that he may direct our intelligence.*

Hinduism is a planetary religion that connects us with the Earth, the Sun, the planets and the stars, not as mere material globes but as centers of life and consciousness. We need such a planetary religion to overcome the present global crisis, which is based upon promoting ethnic, religious, or national differences over the greater planetary good.

Science is showing us how to change the human being physically through genetic manipulation. This remains outer and cannot change the soul. Hinduism through its mantras, rituals and meditations shows us how to change the human being from within, altering negative karmic patterns and creating a higher consciousness as our human birthright. This is the real way forward for humanity.

An era of great transition and change awaits India as well, which is still struggling to free itself from the aftershocks of a thousand years of foreign rule. Only in the last decade has the country started to awaken to its real purpose as a nation. To echo the great Yogi and Seer, Sri Aurobindo, India's destiny is to take her appointed role as the world guru, the spiritual guide and the Divine Mother of nations. But this cannot occur if Hindus reject their great spiritual heritage and embrace inferior creeds. It requires that Hindus take up their spiritual and cultural legacy with both wisdom and vitality. Hopefully my journey can aid in this process and inspire others to complete it.

May Bharat Mata rise once again as the great Earth Mother!

May our worldwide Vedic roots again put forth new luxuriant growths!

May all lands and people restore their heritage of the great rishis and yogis!

# Appendix

# The Meaning of the Term Hindu

In the Vedic Age the land of India was called Sapta Sindhu, the land of the seven rivers. The same name appears in the *Zend Avesta,* the holy book of the ancient Persians, as Hapta Hindu, with the Sanskrit 's' replaced with an 'h', a sound shift that occurs in various Indian dialects as well. The Greeks called the land India or Indika, which also derives from the term Sindhu, removing the initial sound altogether. So clearly Sindhu or Hindu was a name for India going back to very ancient times. India was Sindhu Sthāna, the land of the rivers or Sapta Sindhu Sthāna, the land of the seven rivers.

Sindhu has three meanings in Sanskrit. It means a particular river now called the Sind or Indus, a river in general, or the ocean. Clearly Sindhu in the land of Sapta Sindhu refers to rivers in general and not simply to the Indus as a particular stream only. It meant India as a great land of many rivers. The main river in Vedic India was the Saraswati and in later times became the Ganges. So Sindhu Sthāna is also Saraswati Sthāna and later Ganga Sthāna, not simply the region of the Indus.

Hindu Dharma, Sindhu Dharma or Hinduism is the name of the culture and religions of this great and diverse subcontinent. Hinduism as Sindhu Dharma has three meanings following the meanings of Sindhu.

1.  It is the river religion (Sindhu Dharma). It flows and develops like a river. Not limited by an historical revelation, Hinduism continues to grow and develop through time without losing track of its origins in the eternal.
2.  It is a religion of many rivers, a pluralistic tradition that accepts

the existence of many paths, many sages and many holy books and is always open to more.

3. Sindhu means the ocean. Hinduism is a religion like the ocean that can accept all streams without overflowing. This is also the meaning of Hinduism as Sanātana Dharma or the universal tradition.

Sindhu became Hindu not only among the Persians but also in some dialects in India, particularly in the west of the country. By the twelfth century in the *Prithvīrāj Rāso* by the poet Chand Baradāi, probably the oldest work in the Hindi language, we already find the term Hindu proudly used in India for the religion and people of the region.

Since Hinduism as Sindhu Dharma refers to all the religions and philosophies of India, it naturally includes Buddhist, Jain and other Indic traditions. In this regard Hinduism is not limited to the Vedic tradition and accepts both Vedic and non-Vedic streams.

On the other hand, the Vedic tradition itself is pluralistic and is not limited to existing Vedic paths. It is based on the great Vedic statement, "That which is the One Truth, the sages speak in many ways (*ekam sad viprā bahudhā vadanti*)." The Vedic tradition, therefore, has the basis to integrate all the Dharmas of India including those that regard themselves as non-Vedic.

Yet beyond India, Hinduism can accept all cultures that seek to live in harmony with the universe and respect all creatures. Such a definition would make Hinduism a religion not merely of India but a way of organically adapting the universal truth to the needs of time, place and person everywhere.

Hindu Dharma is a human or Mānava Dharma, encompassing all aspects of human life. It shows what all human beings require for health, happiness, creativity and liberation. May its blessings come to all!

# Index

Advani, L.K., on Indian and Western media vis-a-vis BJP government, 101.

Age of Evangelization, end of, 167-168.

Al Hallaj (Mansur), Sufi dismembered for making Vedantic proclamations, 123.

Alandi, spiritual vibration at, 68.

Alexandria, Christians destroyed great library of, 141.

American Council of Vedic Astrology (ACVA), foundation of, 171.

American culture, revolt against, 32.

American Hinduism, New Age Movement promises to emerge as, 180; not to be scaled down to needs of American commercialism but remain experience of one's Self and true to nature in context of American landscape, 182.

American Institute of Vedic Studies, Vedic Research Centre converted into, 169.

American Protestants, more honest than Catholics in views about Hinduism and their intentions, 165.

American Sufi, places ordinary Muslims above Ramana Maharshi, 124-125.

American Yoga movement, lacks connection with greater Yoga tradition and its Hindu foundation, 178-179; needs exposure to broader culture of Hinduism, 179.

Anandamayi Ma, opens devotional potentials, 47-48.

Anglicans, missionary activity of, 151.

Anti-Hindu media, 74-78; often speaks of 'Hindu fundamentalism', 74; praises Islam and Islamic states, 74-75; praises Marx and Communism and kowtows to (Red) China and Soviet Russia, 75; uncritical embracing of Aryan invasion theory by, 75; invents charges of militance against pacifistic and service oriented Hindu groups, 77; perpetrates deception on uninformed readers and tells deliberate lies, 79-80.

Anti-Hindu Stereotypes, way to overcoming of, 13-15.

Anti-War Movement (in America), involvement in, 35-37.

Apollonius of Tyna, great ancient European mystic, was not a Christian, 139-140.

Aquinas, Thomas, dry and dogmatic philosophy of, 35.

Egypt, ancient, sensing a
monumental spiritual culture
in, 29.

Egyptians, ancient, built pyramids
which reflect cosmic
consciousness and profound
knowledge of occult, 140.

Elst, Koenraad, a Westerner having
a grasp of India better than
Indians, 96.

Eurocentricism, recognizing
distortions born of, 16.

European mystical tradition, older,
contact with, 34.

Evangelical Christians, Veda and
Vedanta regarded as work of
the devil by, 154-55.

Evangelical missionaries,
described as "wolves" by the
Pope for targeting Catholics in
Brazil, 151.

Existentialism, has no solution to
dilemma of existence, 30-31.

Ficino, Marsilio, Renaissance
started as mystical awakening
with, 35.

Francis of Assisi, St., was half a
Pagan, 141.

Freud (Sigmund), Psychology of,
34.

Feuerstein, Georg, joins effort to
highlight findings on ancient
India, 106-107.

Ganapati Muni, identifies Ramana
with God Skanda, 58;
discovers and renames
Ramana, 62; M.P. Pandit
remains unaware of the work
on Vedas of, 63; Vedic scholar
who bridged gulf between
Aurobindo and Ramana, 63-
64; his extensive work on

many forms of the Goddess,
64.

Gandhi, Mahatma, not recognized
by any Christian leader in the
West as God-realized or self-
realized sage, 147.

Gandhi, Sonia, Hindu backlash
against Christian conversions
not caused by her being a
Christian, 163.

Gautier, Francois, disciple of Sri
Aurobindo, eloquent about
need for resurgent Hinduism,
85.

Gāyatrī mantra, the, let us not
forget, 187.

Ghauri, Mohmmed, patron of
prominent Sufis, killed
thousands of Hindus and
destroyed hundreds of Hindu
temples, 124.

Ghaznavi, Mahmud, patron of
prominent Sufis, killed
thousands of Hindus and
destroyed hundreds of Hindu
temples, 124.

global missionary business, largest
multinational business in the
world with billions of dollars
invested in, 148.

Global Vision 2000, important
Hindu event in United States,
117.

Goa Inquisition, worst Christian
atrocity in India, 162.

God, Christian and Islamic view of,
131; of the Old Testament,
131-132; Truth more important
than, 135-136; not property of
a church or belief, 187.

Goddess, the, experience of, 60-61;
and Bhakti Yoga, 64-65.

Goddess tradition of India, sensing
a feminine archetype in, 3.

on respecting *svadharma* of
each individual, 153; so much
misinformation and
disinformation in the world
about, 154; highest goal of,
155; tremendous loss if India
gave up, 156; declared a
religion of darkness by
Southern Baptists of America,
158; will reach real fulfillment
in Christ as per new Catholic
strategy, 165; vehicle for, 174;
can help spiritualize ecology
movement, 176-177; main
practice of, 177; world of
nature permeated by deities
of, 181; suited for all lands and
all people, 181-182; does not
dwell in mere formal social
identity, 183; best religion in
the world, 184; importance of
the vast culture of, 184-185;
guides us how to live in
harmony with nature and
higher consciousness, 186; a
planetary religion, 187; three
meanings of, 188-189;
includes Buddhist, Jain and
other Indic traditions, 189; is
Mānava Dharma embracing all
aspects of human life, 189.
*Hinduism Today*, reports Hindu
Dharma in the broadest sense
from social to spiritual issues,
98; particularly alert on
missionary mischief, 99; forum
for Hindus to communicate
with each other, 99.
Hindus, targeted by many holy
wars, 11; confused by their
own efforts to equate all
religions, 97; not exclusive in
religious, spiritual or cultural
views, 121; Christians refuse to

apologize for what they did to,
150; misinformed about
Hinduism and other religions,
154-155; religious slur still in
vogue against, 159; reasons for
sudden anger against
Christians of, 162-163.
Hindus in U.K., under siege from
Islamic extremism, 18-119;
want to be called Hindus
rather than Indians or South
Asians, 119.
hippie movement, superficial, anti-
intellectual and hedonist, 36.
history books, portray Vedic
people as primitive nomads,
104-105.
human beings, fallen creatures in
Biblical tradition but form a
brotherhood with Gods in the
Vedas, 132.

Ibn El Arabi, Vedantic mysticism
of, 123.
Ibn Warraq, manner of questioning
of old style religion (Islam) by,
1; scrutinizes Islam, 126.
image worship, historical reason
for Jewish rejection of, 128.
India, has maintained best the
spiritual culture of the ancient
world, 6; Yogic culture of, 7;
major counterculture interest
in, 38; freedom to propagate
makes conversion business
very big in, 149.
Indian intellectuals, transferred
their loyalty from London to
Moscow or Beijing but never
placed it in Delhi, 75;
Westernized and alienated
from their own tradition, 84;
conditioned by Marx, Max
Müller or Macaulay, they

mystic traditions eliminated by Christianity and Islam in, 131.

Nehru, Jawaharlal, Prime Minister, Communism favoured by, 92; made India poor and inefficient by adopting Soviet style economy, 123.

Nehru family, promoting family or community interests at the cost of the nation started with, 83.

neo-Paganism, Catholic Church sees threat in worldwide revival of, 143; revives interest in Native American, African, Hawaiian and Australian traditions, 143.

New Age Movement, Christian fundamentalists see threat of Hinduism through, 170-180; a diverse phenomenon in America with promise to emerge as American Hinduism, 180.

*New York Times, The,* intolerance shown towards Hinduism by, 154.

Nietzche, appeal of the atheism of, 30.

non-Biblical beliefs, built in prejudice against, 19.

Non-Resident Indians (NRIs), more supportive of Hindu traditions than Hindus in India, 115-116.

North-East Christians, become progressively alienated from rest of India and seeking to secede, 163.

One God, Biblical tradition of, 131.

One God and One Book, dark age of oppression ushered in by advent of, 137-138; return of reason ended domination of, 138.

Osama bin Laden, spawned by Islamic fundamentalism, 96.

Pagan Rome, tolerant about religion, 140.

Paganism, portrayed as idolatry, superstition and eroticism by Islam and Christianity, 139; Christian rule destroyed and replaced with churches many temples of, 140; Christians destroyed centre of learning and burned books of, 141; Hindu India new model of resurgent, 142; failure of Catholic Church to eliminate, 143.

Pagans, had deep spiritual traditions, 138; rejected by Christianity without understanding, 138-139; Christian oppression of, 140-142.

Pakistan, does not allow (Christian) missionary activity, 149.

Pandit, M.P., contact with and encouragement from, 51-53; attending weekly meditation of, 57-58; remains unaware of Ganapati Muni's work on the Vedas, 63.

Paul (St.), real founder of Christianity who turned a Jewish sect into Roman religion, 130.

Philippines, the, most Catholic and oldest Christian country in Asia remains one of the poorest countries in Asia, 152.

Planet, the future of, 185-187; Hindu Dharma shows how to counter prevailing negative trends emerging upon, 186.

Plato, great philosopher of pre-

appearance in, 78-79; wide range of religious views held by members of, 79.

Rediff Interview, about Pope's visit and recent Christian upsurge in India, 159-167.

religion(s), real problem is exclusive idea of, 17-18; should provide tools for self-realization, 18; Western pattern of, 19; magnifies our *samsakāras* for good or ill, 93; *sāttvika, rājasika* and *tāmasika* nature of, 93-94; can project cosmic forces of light and knowledge or darkness and ignorance, 95; promotes many superstitions in the world today, 135.

Religion and Superstition, 134-136; faith-based religions encourage superstitions and distort mysticism, 134; religions confuse merely human with divine, 135.

religious conversion, no country raised up economically by, 152. See also the Philippines.

religious exclusiveness, bigotry of, belongs to era of colonialism and racism, 167-168.

Renaissance, discovery of, 35.

*Rigveda*, the, images of an inner landscape in, 33; record of great civilization over a long period and vast area, 104; symbolical meaning of deities in, 111-112; path of *mantra yoga* set forth in, 112.

Rilke, German mystic poet, epitomized real mystic poetry, 33.

Rimbaud, French symbolist poet who had a mystic vision, 32-33.

Robertson, Pat, one of the main leaders of fundamentalist Christian groups in America, 151.

Roman Catholic Christianity, original Christianity not represented by, 129; became prominent through Charlemagne and Holy Roman Empire, 130.

Royal Asiatic Society, Bombay, encounter with Westernized intellectuals at, 83-84; Brahmins and Indian gurus in the West maligned by Marxists at, 84.

Rumi, 44; free spirited Sufi, 133.

Russell, Bertrand, manner of questioning old-style religion (Christianity) by, 1.

Sadhu on (Arunachal) Hill, experience of *siddha* gesture from, 61-62.

*Sāmaveda*, the, path of *dhyāna yoga* set forth in, 112.

Saṁskrita Bharati, main Sanskrit organization in India, 175.

Sanai, Mahmud Ghaznavi great hero in Sufi poetry of, 124.

Sanātan Dharma, correct term for Hinduism, 1, 18. See also Hinduism.

Sangha Parivar, knowing about many organizations affiliated with, 70; much more tolerant than even ordinary Christian and Muslim, 77; easily targeted by Westernized media for lack of sophistication in their intellectual presentations, 91.

Sanskrit language, Indian culture rooted in, 11, the language of Gods, 173-175; vehicle for

Consciousness, 45; opens the Vedic vision, 45-46, 48, 49, 51; compared Western scholars to kids playing with marbles outside gates of a temple, 75; can place all Western intellectuals in one corner of his mind, 84; Western academia rejects views on Veda of, 110; path to Vedic Yoga opened out by, 110-111; on India's destiny as world guru, 187.

Sri Aurobindo Ashram and Pondicherry, 56-58; Mother's *shakti* permeates Pondicherry, 56; Mother unfolds as White Goddess Tara, 57.

Sringeri Shankaracharya Math, Vedantic spirit strong at, 67.

Students for a Democratic Society (SDS), split in, 36.

Subrahmanya Swami, a Westerner articulate writer and speaker on Hindu causes, 99.

Sufis, Islamic equivalent of Jesuits, 123; (Islamic) attacks against India guided by organized orders of, 123-124; were involved with major Islamic rulers who killed thousands of Hindus and demolished hundreds of Hindu temples, 124; prominent patrons of, 124; wrongly portrayed as monists in India, 125. See also American Sufi; Aurangzeb; Ghauri, Mohammed; Ghaznavi, Mahmud; Khilji, Alauddin.

Sufism, intolerance and regimentation (of Islam) in, 44.

Surrealists, twentieth century European artistic movement,

examining of, 33.

Swami Narayan Order, the, attending cultural festivals and visiting the temples of, 117-118.

Taliban, spawned by Islamic fundamentalism, 96.

Taoism, special affinity with, 41.

Tilak (Bal Gangadhar), introduced to work of, 70; closely connected with Aurobindo, 70-71.

*Times of India, The*, labels RSS and family as militant fascist, and chauvinistic, 74.

Tiruvannamalai, presence of tremendous spiritual fire in, 58-59; experience of Goddess in, 60.

Transcendental Meditation (TM), contact with, 34.

Transcendentalism in America, Hindu ideas central to development of, 3-4.

Trinidad, significant Hindu presence in, 119.

United Christian Forum for Human Rights, really a forum to promote Christianity, 157.

United States, the, new Evangelical force in the world coming out of, 151.

Upanishads, study of, 34; great inspiration found in, 39; closed the door backward on the more mysterious Vedic age, 49.

Untouchability, excessive pursuit of purity gave rise to, 82-83.

Vajpayee, Atal Behari, Prime Minister, asks for national

Vedic Physics, part of Vedic sciences, 173.

Vedic pluralism, not polytheism but a free and open path with no need to convert, 133.

Vedic Pluralism and Biblical Monotheism, 131-134; Biblical monotheism is exclusivist, 132-133; Vedic view is pluralistic, 132-133.

Vedic Research Centre, foundation of, 169.

Vedic Samaj, development of the idea of, 113, purpose and principles of, 113-114.

Vedic science(s), reconciles outer science to inner truth, 2-3; different branches of, 169; can integrate spiritual sciences with material sciences, 173; firm foundation of, 175.

Vedic tradition, matter of direct experience, not mere belief, 54; emphasizes impersonal (*apaurusheya*) and eternal (*sanātana*), 134-135; has the basis to integrate all dharmas of India, 189.

Vedic *Yajñas*, scientific ways of harnessing secret powers of nature, 175.

Vedic Yoga, following the path of, already opened out by Aurobindo, 111-113.

Vishva Hindu Parishad (VHP), contact with, 70; broadminded people branded narrow fundamentalists in America, 77; asks Pope to apologize for Christian conversions by force, 157.

Vishva Hindu Parishad of America, forum for teaching and defending Hinduism, 115.

Vivekananda, Swami, could place all Western intellectuals in one corner of his mind, 84; sees Mohammed as dangerous mixture of religious insights and religious fanaticism, 124.

Vivekananda Yoga Kendra, Bangalore, visit to, 177.

Voice of India, publishes best series of books in defence of Hindu Dharma, 90-91; controversial because Hindu point of view not articulated previously, 92.

West, the, Hindu ideas permeated to popular consciousness of, 3-4; Ramana Maharshi or Sri Aurobindo or Mahatma Gandhi not honoured as God-realized sage by any leader in, 147; Yogic and Vedantic traditions will be ended by conversion of India by Catholic leaders in, 164; Ayurveda becomes part of alternative medicine in, 170.

West to East, journey from, 6, 7.

Western academia, belief about the Vedas in, 13; gaining the ire of, 110-111; any criticism of Aryan invasion theory dismissed as Hindu politics by, 110; positions used to further their own political and cultural agenda by academics in, 111.

Western gurus, self-proclaimed, spiritual hubris of, 39.

Western influenced media, portray Hindus as intolerant while ignoring Christian violence, 144.

Western intellectuals, fail to answer questions answered by